Ancient Turkey

A Captivating Guide to Göbekli Tepe and the Ancient Civilizations of Anatolia and Eastern Thrace

Free Bonus from Captivating History
(Available for a Limited time)

Hi History Lovers!

Now you have a chance to join our exclusive history list so you can get your first history ebook for free as well as discounts and a potential to get more history books for free! Simply visit the link below to join.

Captivatinghistory.com/ebook

Also, make sure to follow us on Facebook, Twitter and Youtube by searching for Captivating History.

Contents

Introduction

The Republic of Turkey is a fascinating country with an intricate history that makes it one of the most unique countries in the world. It is the home of dynamic cultures and a diverse mix of peoples, which contribute to the elaborate tapestry that attracts thousands of tourists every year. For much of its history, the region that makes up modern Turkey was divided into Anatolia and Eastern Thrace. Anatolia was the Asian part of the region, while Eastern Thrace was the European part. The two regions remained distinct and separate until the Romans conquered the area and united them. In time, Turkey became an important part of the Byzantine Empire. During its long history, Turkey belonged to the Seljuk dynasty and the Ottoman Empire before finally becoming the Republic of Turkey. By then, Turkey consisted of a blend of cultures and influences that all contributed to a distinct way of life.

While Turkey's medieval history is a remarkable field of study, this book will focus on ancient Anatolia and the secrets hidden behind the Roman, Seljuk, and Ottoman influences. Beneath the impressions left by mighty invading empires lies an extraordinary history. The early empires that occupied Anatolia were special and had their own styles of art and religion. This book will equip even complete beginners with a comprehensive insight into ancient Turkey and the people who lived there.

The first part of the book will take a look at Göbekli Tepe, which is a stunning example of what prehistoric life looked like in ancient Turkey. Before mighty warriors and impressive kings, people developed a highly functional settlement that would provide a firm foundation for what was yet to come. After a quick tour of Göbekli Tepe, the development of early Anatolia will be discussed. Ancient Turkey progressed from prehistoric civilizations to the beginning of the mighty region of Anatolia, which would leave its mark on history. The next stop on the exciting tour will shed some light on the Hittite and Mitanni cultures. These people were a serious threat to the Mesopotamian kingdoms, and they have a gripping story to tell.

From the Hittites and Mitanni, the book moves on to the classical Anatolian empires and cultures, such as the Lydian Empire. This kingdom was home to famous kings like Croesus, but it was made up of more than just famous individuals. It had a fascinating culture and society. After the Hittites came the Phrygians, who were led by King Midas. The Phrygian language was part of the Indo-European dialect, which is noteworthy since it displays the ties the Phrygians had with their neighbors. However, the Phrygians weren't the only ones to emerge from the fall of the Hittites. Urartu became a force to be reckoned with for hundreds of years until its own catastrophic fall.

The final part of the book discusses the legacy of ancient Anatolia, such as art, architecture, mythology, and the individuals who made Anatolia great. For better or worse, the kings and emperors of Anatolia either contributed to its rise or fall. The last chapter will focus on these men, such as Gyges, Suppiluliuma, Alyattes, and Priam. They led eventful lives and left behind strong legacies that still draw the attention of scholars and historians. By the end of the book, ancient Anatolia will be slightly less of a mystery. You will know several fascinating topics of conversation or a list of places to visit in the Republic of Turkey.

Most importantly, this book is simple and lays out the history of ancient Turkey in a way that's easy to follow. Discover what influenced the ancient Anatolians and what life was like in the region. Besides focusing on kings, gods, and mythical figures, this book also considers the ordinary people who made their homes in Anatolia. Archaeologists have found notable artifacts that provide valuable insight into what life was like for normal people who wouldn't have their names etched in history. By mixing the stories of powerful and ordinary individuals, this book provides a comprehensive picture of life in ancient Anatolia. It is full of interesting facts that will make history come alive.

Ancient Turkey was a remarkable region that has been occupied since the dawn of history. There is still a lot that historians don't know about the area, but what they have discovered is enough to prompt further investigations. The region might never give up all its secrets, but it certainly is worth exploring.

Chapter 1 – Göbekli Tepe: A Prehistoric Civilization

Located near the Turkish city of Urfa, also known as Şanlıurfa, Göbekli Tepe is an archaeological site that has been called the home of the world's first temple. Göbekli Tepe means "potbelly hill." It was built on a hill that resembles a man with a large belly lying on his back. The site has fascinated historians for years, as it is one of the earliest human settlements. Göbekli Tepe also features the world's oldest megaliths, and its pillars feature decorated reliefs that were likely carved by early Neolithic hunter-gatherers. The area also features other buildings, such as cisterns and quarries from the Neolithic era, which provide invaluable insights into Anatolia's prehistory.

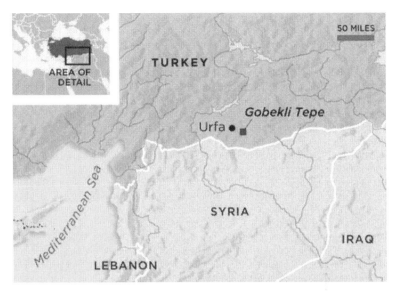

1. Map showing the region where Göbekli Tepe was built

The temple complex itself was built away from convenient water sources, which means it probably wasn't built for farming or agricultural purposes. It is a mysterious site that sometimes leaves historians with more questions than answers. Archaeologists theorize that the site was possibly one of the earliest temples and was used by nomadic hunter-gatherers who gathered intermittently there. Not much is known about the permanent residents of Göbekli Tepe, but what historians have found so far has prompted them to conduct further studies. The site provides a unique insight into the lives of Turkey's earliest residents and is the source of impressive archaeological finds.

Geography

The Göbekli Tepe site is located near the Taurus Mountains in Turkey, which is a range of mountains that separates the Anatolian Plateau from the Mediterranean coast. The mountains stretch from Lake Eğirdir to the Euphrates and Tigris Rivers. Thanks to evidence found at the site, it is clear that humans occupied it between 9600 and 7000 BCE. The site rests on a limestone plateau and is connected to mountains, which means that it is a rocky area filled with sharp slopes.

The area around Göbekli Tepe shows that people interacted with the environment for thousands of years, as historians have found tools and carvings there. There are many caves in the area that early hunter-gatherers might have used as shelters as well.

The limestone plateau was likely chosen since it gave early builders access to plenty of building materials that they used to fashion their tools and build megaliths, some of which still exist. Göbekli Tepe's builders also chose to build their settlement on a high point on the plateau, which gave them a great view of the area. They had access to abundant grasslands, which would have allowed them to harvest grains such as wheat and barley. The grasslands attracted large herds of gazelle, equids, wild sheep, and goats. This meant that the inhabitants of the ancient settlement had access to a variety of food.

There is still some debate as to whether or not the inhabitants of the settlement had easy access to water, as the closest modern springs and streams aren't located near the site. However, the climate of the time, which was likely balmier and rainier, may have allowed for more springs, some of which were likely close to Göbekli Tepe. Archaeologists have also found evidence of cisterns, which meant that the inhabitants of the settlement likely worked out a system to gather rainwater.

The World's First Temple

From its place on the edge of the Fertile Crescent (a particularly fertile strip of land shaped like a crescent that runs from the Persian Gulf to Lebanon, Jordan, Egypt, and Israel), Göbekli Tepe would have been perched on top of paradisaic plains that were filled with rivers, fruit and nut trees, and fields of grazing animals and large amounts of wild grains. It would have attracted hunter-gatherers from all over the region, and as they developed the area, they began to settle down and construct buildings. However, the site doesn't show that people lived there permanently, which leads to an important question. Why would people build an intricate system of megaliths at Göbekli Tepe?

Archaeologists working at the site have theorized that the site was used for religious purposes, while some claim that the area could have been used as the world's first astronomical observatory. A German archaeologist named Klaus Schmidt led the excavations at Göbekli Tepe from 1996 to 2014. He believed that the site was the world's first temple and claimed that archaeologists have barely scratched the surface of what the site holds. When Schmidt's team first began working at the site, they found circular megaliths that were startlingly close to the surface. The intricate circular system of structures immediately drew the interest of archaeologists. As the archaeologists worked, they discovered the absence of permanent habitation. There were no houses or trash pits, which meant that people didn't permanently live at the site. This presented an exciting mystery, and carbon dating proved that the site was built around at least 9000 BCE, making it one of the earliest settlements in human history.

Architecture

The temples at Göbekli Tepe are made of sixteen-ton stone pillars, some of which feature animal reliefs carved into the limestone. These pillars were carved in quarries and then transported up the hill, where they were organized into circular patterns that were deliberately planned and likely ritualistic. While working on the site, ancient builders left behind hundreds of stone tools, such as chisels and knives, that were used to construct the ancient marvel.

2. The Ruins of Göbekli Tepe

The site consists of several enclosures that were all built in a geometric pattern. At first, archaeologists thought the complex was built in stages and that each part functioned independently from the other, but new evidence suggests that this was unlikely. It is possible that the structures all made up a massive complex that functioned at different levels. There may have been a hierarchy or some other system that dictated how the complex functioned.

Most of the pillars were built in a T-shape, and many of the pillars were decorated with carvings. Visitors can see the abstract figures carved into the ancient pillars. The ancient artists evidently took inspiration from the world around them, as the pillars were carved to depict gazelles, snakes, lions, and foxes, all animals that would have been found in the Fertile Crescent at the time. It isn't clear whether or not these animals had religious significance. Archaeologists also found evidence of bones, which may indicate that animal sacrifices and feasts took place at the site, further strengthening the view that Göbekli Tepe was a religious site.

Göbekli Tepe Tell

In archaeology, a tell refers to a mound or small hill that is man-made and made out of the debris of consecutive settlements. As time passed, people at these settlements tended to simply build on top of older buildings which compacted the debris and artifacts below them. Tells are often significant sources of artifacts and information, and Göbekli Tepe was no different. When Klaus Schmidt and his team visited the area in the 1990s, he realized that the mounds weren't naturally occurring and that he had probably stumbled across an ancient tell. He was soon proved right after the excavations started.

The western edge of the site houses an interesting tell that yielded a figure that may have been carved to represent a lion. Historians believe that the area may have been used as some sort of workshop for artisans. The floor was carefully hewn out of stone and smoothed out, which meant that it received a lot of foot traffic and was an important part of the complex. Many of the structures in the tell resemble religious buildings at the neighboring site of Nevalı Çori, which reinforces the idea that the complex was a sacred place. The site features stairs, cisterns, pillars, and benches. The floor plan of the site was well-planned, which is impressive since this was before people used writing to communicate. There are also several rectangular structures within the complex, although their purpose isn't known.

Layer 1

This layer is the closest to the hilltop and shows that the site was used for farming for a long time after the site lost its sacred significance. Once Göbekli Tepe faded into obscurity, the land was farmed mercilessly until it lost its fertility. People likely then moved on to greener pastures. The first layer accounts for the most recent stretch of time and gives archaeologists an idea of what life was like during Göbekli Tepe's later years. In time, the paradise that once housed wild grains and herds of animals became sectioned land that was overworked, as the level of erosion from this layer suggests that the land was used extensively for farming, which would have exhausted its fertility.

When the first hunter-gatherers discovered the area, there were many different kinds of plants and animals, which would have made it perfect for nomadic tribes. They likely would have included the region in their travels, and if the site was indeed a temple, nomadic tribes would have made pilgrimages to the site. It is clear that by 8000 BCE, the development of farming had changed life forever. As nomadic tribes began to settle down, they formed communities, and urban settlements eventually became more common. Suddenly, Göbekli Tepe would have seemed like a relic from a past way of life that no longer held any significance. It is important to note, however, that the site wasn't simply abandoned. The first layer is filled with old stone tools, animal and human bones, and fragments. This means that the site was likely deliberately buried in refuse and soil. For some reason, after 8000 BCE, the inhabitants of the area deliberately filled the site and simply began farming over it.

Layer 2

The second layer of Göbekli Tepe revealed the emergence of rectangular instead of circular structures. As time went on, the builders of the settlement likely realized that rectangular rooms were easier to build and made better use of the available space. However, the second layer's buildings still prominently feature T-shaped pillars, which means that while new building styles had been adopted, the rooms likely still served the same purpose. The buildings of the second layer have been dated back to the period between 8800 and 8000 BCE. The rooms are all windowless but have polished limestone floors, which means the rooms were frequently used. Historians theorize that the rooms may have been used as sanctuaries, which would make sense if the settlement was regarded as a religious site. Each room would have had a specific function in connection with the temple, but not much is known about the settlement's functionality since no written records exist from that time period.

Most of the rooms have tall pillars in the middle featuring carved animals and some human forms. Archaeologists also found totem-like poles buried at Göbekli, which suggests that the animal carvings may have had religious significance. Several totem poles were found at other archaeological sites in Turkey from later periods. Perhaps the old religion was widespread and existed for hundreds of years before eventually fading away as the people became more advanced. Unfortunately, due to the lack of written records, historians have to rely on ancient artifacts to try and piece together the truth about Göbekli Tepe. While the people who used the settlements didn't write anything down, they left behind an abundance of clues to help solve the mystery of their existence.

Layer 3

The third layer is the oldest and features the famous circular structures that have become associated with the mysterious archaeological site. Four such circular enclosures have been uncovered, but surveys have shown that at least sixteen more enclosures still remain buried. The enclosures are made of thick stones with T-shaped pillars set into the walls. Two pillars were set in the middle of each enclosure and were intricately carved with images of animals that were commonly found in the area. It is uncertain whether or not the enclosures had ceilings.

3. A stone carving at Göbekli Tepe

It is apparent that ancient workers used flint points to quarry stone from the surrounding areas and transported the heavy stone slabs up the hill. This was an impressive feat for a civilization that primarily consisted of hunter-gatherer nomadic tribes. The level of organization that went into building the settlement is truly remarkable, and it is clear that the site was very important for a long time. Archaeologists also found a few carvings that were meant to represent human features, such as arms, shoulders, and loincloths, although it is unclear what these features are supposed to symbolize. The circular enclosures have been carbon dated to around 9000 BCE, although it is possible that some of the buried enclosures are older. The smooth stone floors were evidently made first, and builders later made pedestals to support the massive stone pillars that came next.

While it still isn't clear why the enclosures at Göbekli Tepe were built, they are certainly a marvel considering their age and the effort that went into their construction.

Archaeological History

In 1963, the University of Istanbul and the University of Chicago conducted a survey on the hill where Göbekli Tepe is located. The hill is known as Girê Mirazan, which means "sacred hill" in Kurdish.

Unfortunately, that survey yielded few results, as the archaeologists mistook the tops of the pillars for medieval grave markers. A few Neolithic tools were found and reported, but no further investigation was conducted. Since the land had been cultivated for a long time, this means the ground had been disturbed, and some of the pillars were badly damaged by local farmers who likely didn't know the significance of the rocks they were trying to break.

Klaus Schmidt visited the site in 1994, looking for sites like Nevalı Çori. When he stumbled across the survey conducted in 1963, he realized that there might have been more lying beneath the surface. With the help of local farmers and villagers, he found the site. Mahmut and Ibrahim Yıldız owned the land and found several artifacts they handed over to the local museum. Schmidt quickly began working on the site and discovered the ancient megaliths. He worked on the site on behalf of the German Archaeological Institute and Şanlıurfa Museum until his death in 2014.

Work has continued at the site, but the goal has changed somewhat. While many enclosures still remain buried, the main focus has been preservation and conservation. This is vital work, as the ancient site is slowly being exposed to the elements, which could seriously damage the megaliths.

Conservation

In an effort to preserve the site from the elements and further human interference, the Global Heritage Fund (GHF) supports a conservation program to protect Göbekli Tepe. The GHF has partnered with the German Research Foundation, the German Archaeological Institute, the Turkish Ministry of Tourism and Culture, and the Şanlıurfa government. In addition to building a protective roof over the site, the conservation plan includes training and educating locals about archaeology and conservation. Göbekli Tepe was also added to the UNESCO World Heritage List in 2018.

The shift in focus from excavation to conservation means that work has slowed down considerably at the site. However, it is important to preserve what has already been found, as it would be reckless to continue digging without protecting the ancient buildings that have already been exposed. Göbekli Tepe will continue to receive attention from archaeologists and scholars due to its age and significance, but that attention could also lead to more damage. The site is open to the public, and a large walkway was built around some excavated areas. This stirred up controversy, as some archaeologists feared that the construction of the walkway would result in problems at the site.

4. Walkway and roof protecting the ruins at Göbekli Tepe

Ever since the enclosures were excavated, weather conditions proved to be a problem since the site lacked proper drainage. Several other problems became apparent, which convinced archaeologists that before any more major excavations took place, the site needed to be protected. Some areas are being excavated under steel covers, which protect the artifacts from the weather. Lee Clare, a coordinator at the site, explained that large-scale excavations lead to destruction and that future digs will be more limited. The goal is to carefully catalog all the finds at the site so that Göbekli Tepe will continue to survive for future generations.

Restoration Efforts

Göbekli Tepe revolutionized the way that archaeologists theorized that civilizations developed. In the past, it was suggested that hunter-gatherer tribes settled down once they learned how to farm. Once they had a surplus of food, they were able to create complex societies, which then led to the rise of kingdoms and empires. However, Göbekli Tepe was built long before the advent of agriculture, which suggests that something else drew the nomadic tribes together and convinced them to settle down. Klaus Schmidt was convinced that the site was the world's first temple and that humans were drawn together because of their love of a spectacle. He theorized that the site's location meant that Göbekli Tepe was mankind's first "cathedral on a hill." It would have been a spectacular sight since it overlooked the rich and vibrant fields that consisted of several different species of animals. The structure would have faced the lush fields, and it would have been a marvel of engineering for its time.

Unfortunately, over the years, the land was dedicated to farming and overworked to the point where it became less vibrant and fertile. In recent years, the area has faced a refugee crisis due to the Syrian conflict, which has led to a sharp downturn in tourism. In an effort to draw more visitors to the ancient site, Turkey has decided to restore some of the features of the enclosures. Turkey's Doğuş Group partnered with the National Geographic Society and announced its intention to spend millions of dollars to preserve and restore the site.

Klaus Schmidt theorized that as hunter-gatherer tribes met to build the site, they invented agriculture to feed and sustain the large workforce that was needed to build it. Göbekli Tepe is an ancient marvel that has made historians question the way they look at the ancient world, but the site is shrouded in mystery and is unlikely to give up all its secrets any time soon.

Chapter 2 – Early Anatolia

Anatolia is a diverse region with an interesting history. Over hundreds of years, several cultures and kingdoms rose to prominence before falling into extinction. Some of the most interesting kingdoms include the Hittite and the Mitanni, which dominated the region before they were defeated. In time, the Lydian Empire became the strongest power and left behind an impressive legacy. There are still many stories that Anatolia has yet to tell, as much of its history has been hidden beneath the surface. Historians have their work cut out for them as they try to piece together all the parts of Anatolia's rich history.

While many cultures left behind written records and myths before they collapsed, some of Anatolia's inhabitants only left a few clues behind. Much of Anatolia's prehistory is still unknown, but there are remains of ancient settlements and villages that provide insight into the lives of the people who built megaliths, developed religions, and learned to work with tools. The history of Anatolia's mighty kingdoms is gripping, but its prehistory is perhaps more interesting because of all the questions that still haven't been answered. Beginning with the Stone Age and traversing through the murky Neolithic, Chalcolithic, and Bronze Ages, Anatolia's prehistory provides context for the climatic rise and fall of its later empires.

Stone Age (c. 10,000–5500 BCE)

The Stone Age refers to the period in mankind's history before people began working with metal to make tools. There are several time periods within the Stone Age, including the Paleolithic, Mesolithic, and Neolithic periods. The Stone Age lasted until about 5500 BCE, when the Chalcolithic Age (or Copper Age) began. Historians have found evidence that people resided in ancient Anatolia from Paleolithic times. A stone tool was found in the Gediz River that has been dated back to about a million years ago, and there are a number of sites in Turkey that reveal evidence of Paleolithic habitation.

5. Yarımburgaz Cave

One of the most interesting Paleolithic sites is the Yarımburgaz Cave in Istanbul. The cave is made out of natural limestone and has attracted archaeologists and scientists due to its status as an important fossil site. Archaeologists have found artifacts from the Paleolithic era, which suggests that people may have inhabited the cave during colder seasons. Recently, geologists have found new galleries deeper in the cave that weren't used by humans since they are too difficult to reach. During the Byzantine era, the cave was turned into a chapel and monastery, which increased its value to historians. Unfortunately, the cave has been badly damaged and vandalized in recent years. The site hasn't been properly protected, and its proximity to the bustling metropolis of Istanbul means that its easily accessed by locals and tourists. The cave has also been used as a set in several Turkish films and television series, which led to Byzantine frescoes being damaged.

The Paleolithic Age was a time when humans were hunter-gatherers and roamed the land looking for food. However, that era gave way to the Mesolithic period, during which mankind began to develop agriculture and settle down into more organized societies. Several caves in Turkey, as well as ancient sites along the Black Sea and Mediterranean coast, have yielded proof of Mesolithic settlements in ancient Anatolia.

Neolithic Age (c. 8000–5500 BCE)

Until the 1960s, historians assumed that Anatolia remained uninhabited until the Copper Age and spent most of their energy focusing on the Fertile Crescent, which has been called the cradle of civilization. However, all of that changed when they found evidence of ancient settlements dating to around 8000 BCE that revealed a distinct lack of pottery and domesticated animals. This meant that people lived in Anatolia before they mastered agriculture and still used stone tools.

Around that time, people built simple houses out of mudbricks and plastered their walls and floors. They learned how to farm barley and wheat but still had a lot of development ahead of them. One of the most notable sites can be found at Hacilar, which also housed the remains of Chalcolithic artifacts. Historians discovered that these ancient people painted their walls and lived in an organized society.

However, Hacilar was abandoned for about a thousand years before people returned to the settlement.

For years, historians struggled to make an accurate archaeological record of the transition from the Neolithic period to the Chalcolithic Age. Thankfully, the discovery of ancient settlements helped them to fill the gaps. The investigation of these settlements has shed light on the lives of the ancient Anatolians. Two of the most important sites are Nevalı Çori, which was an early Neolithic settlement located near Göbekli Tepe, and Çatalhöyük, which was a relatively advanced city-like settlement that bridged the gap between the Neolithic and Chalcolithic periods.

Nevalı Çori

Nevalı Çori was likely built during the early Neolithic era and can be found in the modern-day Sanlıurfa province in Turkey near the site of Göbekli Tepe. It's an ancient settlement that holds a lot of interest for archaeologists and scientists since evidence of the world's earliest domesticated einkorn wheat was found at the site. Unlike Göbekli Tepe, it appears as though people lived at Nevalı Çori and built homes for themselves. The homes were built out of stones that were packed tightly together. Most of these structures had gaps under the floors where channels were built. Historians theorize that the ancient homes were built with functional drainage systems or that the channels were used to cool the houses down.

6. Temple uncovered at Nevalı Çori

While it's clear that there are many differences between the sites of Nevalı Çori and Göbekli Tepe, there are a few similarities. A section of the settlement contains the same type of pillars found at Göbekli Tepe. The pillars bear the same shape and are set into the walls of a complex that seems to have had religious significance to the residents of the ancient town. There is also an abundance of limestone at Nevalı Çori, which ancient builders and artisans used to carve reliefs and sculptures. Historians have found hundreds of clay figures that were carved to resemble animals and humans. Some of the pillars at Nevalı Çori depict similar carvings to the pillars at Göbekli Tepe. Archaeologists also discovered a sculpture of a life-sized human head, and for some reason, pillars at Nevalı Çori were decorated with carvings of human hands.

It isn't clear what the purpose of the carvings and figurines was, but some of the artwork provide an insight into life at Nevalı Çori. Historians have found fascinating carvings depicting hunting expeditions. While scholars may never know everything about Nevalı Çori, there's enough evidence to piece together a good idea of what life might have been like for the inhabitants of the ancient site.

Çatalhöyük

The ancient city of Çatalhöyük has been around for thousands of years and was used by the ancient Romans about two thousand years ago, but the city itself dates as far back as 7500 BCE. It is an endlessly fascinating site, with some of the most important clues about what life was like in Anatolia during the Neolithic era. While the settlement was occupied by Greeks and Romans for a long time, archaeologists mostly focus on the impact of the prehistoric people who made their home there. Evidence of ancient mudbrick houses has been found. Not only did prehistoric people build the large settlement, but they also took the time to paint and decorate their homes. The homes also served as tombs and memorials, as deceased family members were buried under the homes.

7. Ruins of Çatalhöyük

Archaeologists have been working on the site since the 1960s and have found thousands of artifacts that revolutionized our view of prehistoric Anatolia. While the earliest inhabitants of Çatalhöyük didn't leave behind any written records, they left behind clues about their bustling small city. It seems evident that the residents of the settlement engaged in trading with communities from the Mediterranean and Red Seas, which would have been an incredible feat at the time.

While the site has provided a lot of insight into prehistoric life, it also raised many questions. For example, many of the earliest homes show that the people lived relatively equal lives. There's no evidence of a religious or administrative center, and most houses had the same amount of goods and were the same size. All of this points to a relatively equal society, but some of the skulls uncovered at the site show similar head wounds. This means that people were struck in the head but lived after they healed from their injuries, which means they were likely stunned for some reason. Perhaps the inhabitants of the settlement captured people from outside the settlement to serve as slaves or wives. Unfortunately, it may be a long time before the secrets of Çatalhöyük are fully explained.

Chalcolithic Age (c. 5500–3000 BCE)

While the Stone Age is defined as a period when mankind began working with stone tools, the Chalcolithic era tells of a time when mankind began working with metal implements, namely copper. This is a particularly noteworthy stage in mankind's history since it marks the transition from the Neolithic to the Bronze Age. Archaeologists believe that the rise of the Copper Age may have begun in the Fertile Crescent. The earliest evidence of metalworking was found in Yarim Tepe, which can be found in Iraq. This evidence led scholars to believe that prehistoric people began working with lead before they moved on to smelting copper. As people became better at working with metal, they left behind stone tools and entered a new era.

There are many sites in Anatolia that shed light on the Chalcolithic Age in Anatolia, but one of the most important can be found at Hacilar.

Hacilar

Hacilar was an ancient settlement that has been dated back to about 7000 BCE, and evidence shows that the settlement was inhabited intermittently during its long history. Structures and artifacts show that settlers were living at the site when the Neolithic era came to an end and the Chalcolithic Age began. Early homes were made out of mudbrick, and the upper floors may have been made out of wood. The ceilings were generally flat, and walls were plastered and decorated with paint or figurines. The most prominent designs were red shapes painted onto cream backgrounds; this style was used to decorate a lot of the pottery that was found at the site. As time progressed, houses were built to include workshops, storage spaces, and stoves. Since no doors have been found on the ground levels of these homes, archaeologists think they were accessed from the roof.

It also seems that the first temple was built at the site at the beginning of the Chalcolithic era. Besides the sacred elements that were added, it seems the villagers saw a need to protect themselves since the settlement was fortified around that time too. Historians have found evidence that the people who lived at Hacilar were mostly farmers and had begun working with grains such as wheat and barley. They had also begun breeding domestic animals such as cattle and sheep before the Chalcolithic period. As time went on, their sculptures became more advanced, and many of the figurines represented animals and nude females. It is possible that the figurines represented their gods or goddesses.

Bronze Age (c. 3300–1200 BCE)

The earliest phase of the Bronze Age was made up of the Copper Age, but scholars use that term less since it created confusion in the past. It is important to note that the Chalcolithic Age is a distinct term, but some scholars prefer to refer to that age as the Early Bronze Age. As people began working with metal, they found that they could sometimes make stronger tools by adding different elements. In time, copper work gave way to bronze work. This led to the Bronze Age, which would be marked by remarkable developments in culture and society. Anatolia wasn't immune to the changes that took place during the Bronze Age, and several civilizations benefited greatly from the developments that swept through the region.

The Bronze Age is a large period of time that has been divided into three separate periods: the Early, Middle, and Late Bronze Ages. One of the most important settlements during the Early Bronze Age was the settlement of Büyükkaya, which later became the prominent city of Hattusa or Hattush. This was where the Hattians made their home; later, the Hittites took control and made it their capital. Anatolians found metal deposits in this region, which allowed them to work extensively with metals. This allowed them to trade with other areas, including the mighty Akkadian Empire in Mesopotamia.

Moreover, the Bronze Age saw the rise of cultures that were adopted by many different civilizations, which means that people were traveling and sharing their customs. One of the most notable cultures from this period was the Kura-Araxes culture.

The Bronze Age was a remarkable time in human history, and it provides a lot of insight into some of the most influential civilizations that arose in Anatolia. The advent of metallurgy forever changed the course of history, and ancient Anatolia provides some valuable insights into the time period.

Kura-Araxes Culture

The Kura-Araxes culture is also known as the Early Transcaucasian culture, and it began around 4000 BCE before disappearing two thousand years later. At its height, it stretched from the South Caucasus to eastern Turkey, Syria, northwestern Iran, and the northeastern Caucasus region. Scholars theorize that the distinctive culture began in the Caucasus area and was later mixed with foreign elements that all became one culture. The people in these regions would have shared a similar culture that would have united them and helped to develop a society. Most houses during this period were simple and made from mudbricks. At first, houses were round, but they later became rectangular. Most people of the Kura-Araxes culture were farmers and worked with grain and domesticated animals.

8. Kura-Araxes pottery and ax-head

However, their most notable achievement was their pottery. The Kura-Araxes culture is defined by their red and black pottery that features intricate geometric designs. These beautiful pieces were transported to far-flung regions like Syria, Chechnya, and Dagestan, which is a testament to the Kura-Araxes culture's influence. Highly skilled artisans would have crafted the pottery and sold it to traders, who would have taken the pieces of art with them as they traveled along the extensive trade routes.

While the Kura-Araxes culture was distinctive and endured for many years, there is an interesting lack of unity in certain areas. It appears as though they didn't have set burial customs, which is unusual. Scholars theorize that the culture developed slowly and had many external influences instead of set customs and rituals. However, as the culture spread and time went on, certain customs became more widespread.

Hattians

The Hattians lived in central Anatolia and occupied the area from around 2300 BCE to 630 BCE. They were highly influential and used a cuneiform script to trade with neighboring civilizations. During their time, the region was filled with forests, which allowed the Hattians to become master woodworkers. They built their homes out of wood and traded with wood and ceramics. It appears as though they worshipped a mother goddess and relied heavily on their goddess to ensure their crops succeeded.

The Hattians were mainly farmers who worked with grains and sheep. Scholars have found evidence that they worked with wool and traded woolen clothing and blankets. While there were many wild animals in the area, the Hattians didn't make a practice of hunting. This is likely due to the fact that they believed that everything had a spirit. They didn't want to risk upsetting their patron goddess. As time went on, the Hattians began to trade with Mitanni, Babylonia, Egypt, and Assyria, which gave them access to exotic resources and a lot of money.

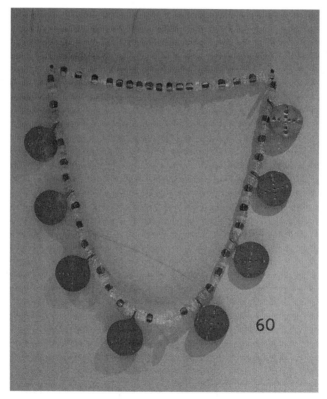

9. Hattian necklace

The Hattians established a mighty capital in Hattusa, where they were able to develop their own language and art. Their capital was built on a massive hill, which made it difficult for others to conquer.

The Akkadians tried to conquer the Hattians on several occasions but failed. Despite several battles with the Akkadians, the Hattians managed to prosper. Unfortunately, the Hittites conquered the city around 1700 BCE, and the Hattian culture began a steady decline. In time, the Hittites managed to gain control of all the Hattian lands, and the two cultures merged into one.

While the Hattians were defeated, there is no doubt that they were a highly influential culture that traded with some of the most powerful kingdoms of their time. They didn't survive the Hittites, but the Hittite culture was heavily influenced by the Hattian culture and was never the same again. While the Hittites became one of the most powerful kingdoms in Anatolia, the Hattians left a mark on history that would not soon be forgotten.

Iron Age (c. 1300-600 BCE)

The Bronze Age was generally a prosperous time, as people learned to make the most of their metal tools. Great civilizations rose and fell, but eventually, the Bronze Age collapsed once people began working with iron and steel. However, the Iron Age wasn't simply marked by inventions in tools and metallurgy. It was also a time when people began to develop literature and writing. Different cultures defined their alphabets, and writing became an important part of civilization. As the Bronze Age ended, the Hittite Empire collapsed and was replaced by other powers who were defined by the advancements of the Iron Age. For example, western Anatolia was occupied by the Lydians, Carians, Lycians, Ionians, and the people of the Troad. Meanwhile, other parts of Anatolia were controlled by the Phrygians, Cimmerians, Assyrians, and Urartians.

The Iron Age saw mighty kingdoms gain power, and in time, the Greeks and Romans took control, which led to a new age in Anatolian history. During this time, kings and emperors made their mark on Anatolia and left behind a diverse history. For example, the Troad housed the legendary city of Troy, which still occupies a space in the imagination of the general public. The Lydians and Phrygians would form influential cultures, while Urartu was the epitome of the classical Anatolian period. Ancient Anatolia was an interesting place, but it is still shrouded in mystery. Once the Bronze and Iron Ages began, Anatolia's history became less of a mystery and more of a record of classical empires.

Chapter 3 – The Hittites and the Mitanni

At one point in Anatolian history, the Hittites and Mitanni oversaw major empires that controlled the culture and economy of the area. These kingdoms were developed over hundreds of years and had dealings with some of the most powerful empires in the world. The Hittites and Mitanni fought against each other and traded with the Assyrian and Egyptian states. They were dominant powers in the region and had a massive impact on Anatolian history.

The Hittites became a force to be reckoned with when they established their new empire in the city of Hattusa during the latter half of the 1600s BCE. They became a powerful empire that went on to conquer large territories. However, they couldn't always govern their newly won lands, which led to power vacuums, and some believe that the Mitanni took advantage of this situation. When the Mitanni developed into a formidable kingdom, the Hittites had to deal with a serious threat that would continue to cause trouble for many years.

While the Hittites were engaged in many wars, they were also involved in the world's first peace treaty and fostered prosperous relationships that benefited both their empire and their allies.

Following the history of these two fascinating cultures will provide a deeper and more complete understanding of ancient Anatolia.

The Hittites

The Hittites first began to appear around 1700 BCE, and it is possible that they developed from the Hatti culture. They ruled over most of Anatolia and parts of Mesopotamia, which made them one of the most powerful empires of their time. In fact, they were a serious threat to the Egyptians until the Hittites signed the peace treaty after the Battle of Kadesh. The Hittites had a definite impact on the kingdoms around them and are frequently mentioned in the Old Testament of the Bible. They were known for repeatedly attacking surrounding nations, which included the Israelites.

10. Hittite sculpture

Their empire endured for hundreds of years, but eventually, they were defeated by the Assyrians. While the Hittites ruled for many years, the empire only reached its peak during the reign of King Suppiluliuma I, who ascended the throne around 1344 BCE and ruled during the period in Hittite history known as the New Kingdom. There are three distinct periods during Hittite history: the Old Kingdom, the Middle Kingdom, and the New Kingdom. Most historians don't count the Middle Kingdom since it refers to a brief period in Hittite history that fell between the Old and New Kingdoms.

During that time, the Hittites experienced about a century of turmoil or a "dark age."

For most of history, the Hittites' past was shrouded in mystery, and they were only mentioned in the biblical record. However, the Hittites left behind thousands of written records that were eventually unearthed by missionaries and archaeologists in the late 1800s CE. These records provide a comprehensive guide to Hittite history, beginning with the Old Kingdom.

The Old Kingdom

It is generally accepted that the Hittites arrived in Anatolia during the Bronze Age. During this time, the Hattians and Hurrians occupied the region, but they were defeated by the Hittites. The Hattians built the city of Hattusa around 2500 BCE, and it became a stronghold for the culture, which managed to resist attacks from the Akkadians. It was conquered by King Anitta, who then proceeded to destroy the city. According to legends of the time, King Anitta placed a curse on Hattusa to prevent people from trying to rebuild the city. However, King Hattusili I later decided to rebuild the city; he has been accredited with founding the Hittite kingdom.

An ancient record from the time (around 1600 BCE) named "The Edict of Telepinus" claims that Hattusili I was a capable warrior who conquered vast lands. He would then leave one of his sons to take care of the newly won lands and continue on to find new territories. It is clear that Hattusili wanted to create a grand unified kingdom that would be ruled by his family, but in time, his sons faced serious rebellions. It is unclear whether his sons were part of these rebellions or were killed, but when it was time for Hattusili to choose an heir, he chose his grandson, Mursili.

Mursili continued his grandfather's wars but didn't seem interested in expanding the kingdom's borders. Instead, he would attack a territory, take all the valuables, and return to Hattusa. During his reign, he successfully looted and destroyed the cities of Aleppo and Babylon. In time, he was assassinated by his brother-in-law, Hantili, who ruled for about three decades. This sparked a trend among Hittite kings, as the next few kings were assassinated.

For the next few decades, the Hittite kingdom fell apart as kings were assassinated or ruled poorly. The last king of the Old Kingdom, Telepenus (also spelled Telepinus), recorded the decline of the once-great kingdom and lived until about 1500 BCE, which marked the beginning of the Middle Kingdom.

The Middle Kingdom

Unfortunately, very few records exist about the Hittite kingdom during its "dark age." This is due to the fact that they were always under attack, mostly from the Kaskians, a group of people who occupied the area by the Black Sea. The Hittites were forced to move their capital a few times and left behind arches and records at Sapinuwa and Samuha, two cities that served as the Hittites' capital during this period. During this time, the Hittites seemed to have preferred negotiating treaties and trying to make peace with their neighbors. Historians have accredited them as being one of the first nations to practice international diplomacy. It's possible that since the Hittites were in no position to conquer other territories, they were forced to turn to diplomacy for survival. These treaties likely helped them to survive the various attacks from the Kaskians.

Not much is known about the ordinary Hittite people or their culture since records from these early periods mostly focused on kings and their accomplishments (or lack thereof). During the Old Kingdom, the king was seen as merely human, unlike other kingdoms where the monarchy was associated with the divine. The Hittites also didn't have firm succession laws. This led to a series of assassinations and coups, which severely destabilized the kingdom.

It is very difficult to try and translate the records left behind by the Hittites. While they used the Akkadian script, they wrote in their own language, which has proved to be frustrating for archaeologists. At first, they could read the words inscribed on the records but couldn't understand what was written. It's possible that the Hattians were influenced by Akkadian and that the Hittites then incorporated several Hattian-Akkadian elements into their culture.

The New Kingdom

The period known as the New Kingdom in Hittite history began with the ascension of King Suppiluliuma I, who became king around 1344 BCE. One of the first things he did was unite the existing Hittite territories and fortify Hattusa. As soon as he was confident that his kingdom was safe, he began expanding its borders. During his reign, he conquered Mitanni and much of the Middle East. He was a capable king and warrior. He also took land from Syria and Egypt, which made him a serious threat to neighboring kingdoms. In fact, the king of Egypt, Akhenaten, and his successor, Tutankhamun, fought against the Hittites but kept losing lands.

11. King Suppiluliuma I

When Tutankhamun died, his wife, Ankhesenamun, requested to marry one of Suppiluliuma's sons. This was an unprecedented arrangement, but Suppiluliuma agreed and sent his son, Zannanza, to marry the queen of Egypt. Zannanza never made it to his destination and was likely murdered by Tutankhamun's general Horemheb or the vizier Ay. Suppiluliuma was enraged and began conquering much of the Levant. Unfortunately for the Hittites, he died from the plague in 1322 and left behind his heir, Arnuwanda II, who also died from the same plague. This left Suppiluliuma's grandson, Mursili II, as the new king of the Hittites.

Mursili was a young man when he took the throne, but he quickly proved his worth when he strengthened the Hittite borders and defeated the Kaskians. He reigned for almost thirty years and left a strong kingdom to his son, Muwatalli II, who would face Ramesses the Great at the Battle of Kadesh.

Battle of Kadesh

Ramesses II was one of Egypt's greatest leaders, and he is accredited with bringing peace and prosperity to Egypt. The Battle of Kadesh is seen as one of his most notable accomplishments, but it didn't end with a decisive victory. Instead, it ended with a revolutionary act: a peace treaty. In fact, the Treaty of Kadesh is considered to be the world's first peace treaty since previous treaties focused on setting borders or were mostly focused on deities.

By the time Ramesses II became king, the Hittites had become a serious threat to Egypt. They had conquered a lot of territories and regularly attacked Egyptian lands.

12. Wall showing the Battle of Kadesh

Ramesses II's predecessors, including Horemheb, had tried to eradicate the Hittites but were unsuccessful. Ramesses II was forced to gather an army in 1274 BCE at the fortified city of Kadesh. However, Ramesses II was overconfident and quickly marched ahead of his main army. Muwatalli II was already waiting at Kadesh with a massive army and chariots that outnumbered Ramesses II's forces. Ramesses II frantically ordered the rest of his army to join him, and fierce fighting ensued.

Muwatalli II managed to keep Kadesh, but Ramesses II defeated a large portion of the Hittite army. As a result, both kings claimed to have won the battle, but the truth was that the battle ended in a draw. Muwatalli II died shortly thereafter in 1272 BCE, and his son, Mursili III, ascended the throne. Soon, the Hittites and Egyptians realized that neither would gain the advantage over the other and that peace would be the smartest option. In 1258 BCE, the two kings signed the Treaty of Kadesh. As a result, both kingdoms shared their knowledge. The Hittites helped the Egyptians with metalworking, and the Egyptians helped the Hittites become better farmers. It was a mutually beneficial arrangement that improved both countries until the Hittite Empire eventually fell.

The Decline of the Hittites

By the time Hattusili III died, the Assyrians were becoming a formidable power in Mesopotamia, and around 1245, the Hittites and Assyrians clashed at the Battle of Nihriya. Unfortunately for the Hittites, they didn't just have to deal with the Assyrians; they also had to fend off attacks from neighboring tribes. The Hittites lost the Battle of Nihriya, and their empire began a steady period of decline. The Hittite Empire had already experienced its peak, and there wouldn't be another golden era.

In 1210 BCE, King Suppiluliuma II engaged in the first recorded naval battle in history. It was a momentous event, and the Hittites experienced a massive victory over the Cypriots. The victory wasn't enough to save the empire, however. Suppiluliuma II would be the last Hittite king. The Assyrians and the Kaskians kept attacking the Hittites until 1190, when the Kaskians conquered Hattusa and destroyed the city. The Assyrians then looted what they could from the remains of the empire and quickly conquered most of the Hittites' territories. It didn't take long for the Assyrians to completely stamp out the Hittite culture. Soon, the Hittites were obscured by Assyrian history.

The Mitanni

Although the Mitanni weren't as famous as some of their contemporaries, they were one of the greatest nations of their time and were respected by their neighbors. While historians don't know a lot about the ancient culture, a few key records remain that tell the story of a powerful nation that existed between 1500 and 1240 BCE. Some of the letters exchanged by the Mitanni, Assyrian, and Egyptian kings still exist, which proves that Mitanni was one of the most powerful nations of its time.

13. Mitanni cylinder seal

The Mitanni ruled over the northern section of the Euphrates and Tigris Rivers. It has been theorized that the kingdom was ruled by a class of warriors known as *maryannu*, which would explain the origins of their name, but they were also known as the Naharin, the Hanigalbat, and the Hurrians by different nations. Their capital was Washukanni, which occupied an advantageous position on the banks of the Khabur River, which is connected to the Euphrates.

During its peak, the Mitanni kingdom had extensive trade routes along the Euphrates that ran down to Carchemish. This put them in contact with many other Anatolian states and allowed the kingdom to prosper financially. Historians found the world's oldest horse training manual while excavating artifacts at Hattusa. It was written by a Mitanni named Kikkuli. Besides horse training, the Mitanni were accomplished warriors who developed weapons and tactics that gave them the upper hand on the battlefield.

Unfortunately, there aren't many surviving Mitanni records, which means that not much is known about the general populace. However, it is clear that Mitanni was a powerful nation that was renowned for its charioteers and horsemen.

Mitanni Kings

There isn't a lot of information about most of the Mitanni kings, but the records that exist tell an interesting story. Mitanni was a powerful nation that was often at odds with its neighbors. This was largely due to the fact that some of the early Mitanni kings were interested in expanding their borders. One such conflict took place when Thutmose III fought against the Mitanni at Aleppo sometime in the 1400s BCE when the two nations tried to take control of Syrian territory. Several Mitanni kings also tried to create treaties with Egypt through royal marriages, but most of those treaties didn't last long.

Historical records claim that Mitanni experienced a golden age under King Shuttarna II during the 14th century BCE. Thanks to the Amarna Letters, which are Akkadian literature about Egypt's dealings with some neighboring states, historians have been able to gain insight into previously elusive cultures like the Mitanni. These letters detail some important events during Shuttarna II's and his son, Tushratta's, life. One of these events is the marriage of Tushratta's daughter, Tadu-Hepa, to Amenhotep III in an effort to cement a treaty between the two nations. It has been suggested that Tadu-Hepa may have been the famous Egyptian queen, Nefertiti, but it's also likely that she was Akhenaten's other wife, Kiya. The kings sent each other many gifts, such as gold, fabric, jewelry, and camel litters, as they negotiated the marriage contract.

Unfortunately, the treaty wouldn't last. The Mitanni king quickly realized that he didn't receive as much gold as was promised in exchange for the princess, which may have strained relations between the two countries. To make matters worse, Tushratta was locked in a battle against a possible relative, a man named Artatama II. The Hittites meddled in the standoff and supported Artatama II's coup. At first, Tushratta had the upper hand, but that quickly changed when Egypt withdrew its support. Tushratta was assassinated by his son, and the Hittites turned Mitanni into their vassal state.

Mitanni vs. Assyria

Mitanni never recovered from the Hittite invasion, and the nation was divided into two separate provinces. The Hittites referred to their new territory as Hanigalbat and dominated it for years until the Assyrian Empire took control of the nation. It isn't clear when Mitanni fell to the Assyrians, but it has been theorized that the Assyrian King Adad-nirari I invaded the region sometime during his reign. The conquest of Mitanni was completed by his successor, Shalmaneser I. While that theory hasn't been proven, it is clear that Mitanni was definitely defeated before the decline of the Hittite Empire.

Assyrian King Adad-nirari I created records that explained why he conquered Mitanni. According to the king, the Hittite king, Shattuara I, insulted the Assyrian king, which led to a brutal response. Adad-nirari I destroyed the Mitanni and took Shattuara I back to Assur as a prisoner. The Mitanni didn't give up and rebelled against Assyrian rule during the reign of Shalmaneser I, who brutally subdued the Mitanni. The Assyrian king killed the Mitanni army and had the survivors blinded. He quickly destroyed most of the Mitanni cities and attacked Mitanni's allies. The Mitanni were sold as slaves. Soon afterward, the Hittites were conquered, and the Assyrians did their best to destroy any part of the Mitanni culture. The survivors of this brutal conquest were absorbed into the Assyrian Empire, which put a permanent end to the Mitanni.

Legacies of the Hittites and Mitanni

The Assyrian Empire was a powerful force that took no mercy on its enemies. Unfortunately for the Hittites and Mitanni, they made an enemy out of the most powerful empire in the world at that time. The Assyrians didn't take kindly to threats and made sure to wipe out any trace of the Hittites and Mitanni. Due to the efforts of the Assyrians, historians have had to piece together whatever evidence still exists about those once-great nations. It hasn't been an easy task, and for thousands of years, few people knew that the Hittites and Mitanni had ever existed. Their way of life, language, and culture were lost to time. Even though their existence has been brought to light, their cultures have been shrouded in mystery, and very little is known about those kingdoms.

14. Lion Gate at Hattusa

Thanks to ancient records that were stored elsewhere, such as the Amarna Letters, or the artifacts that were recovered from the rubble of Hattusa and other ancient cities, archaeologists are able to find traces of the Hittites and Mitanni. What little evidence still exists about these two nations paints a picture of prosperous and powerful kingdoms. They once rivaled some of the greatest kingdoms of their time. In fact, the Hittites were a serious threat to Egypt until they became one of Egypt's allies. Their impact on Anatolian history is clear, and they helped the people of the region become vastly rich and influential. The Hittites and Mitanni were mighty nations that won't soon be forgotten again.

Chapter 4 – Classical Anatolia: The Lydian Empire

Lydia was a mighty kingdom in western Anatolia that rose to power in the Late Bronze Age. The kingdom existed from about 1200 BCE to 546 CE, and it had a deep impact on Greek and Ionian culture. It was an impressive nation that became rich thanks to its abundant natural resources and advantageous geographic position, which allowed the Lydians to benefit from the extensive trade routes that ran from the Mediterranean to Asia. The Lydians had their own distinctive language and culture that dominated the region while Lydia was still an independent nation. It reached its peak during the Mermnad dynasty, which produced famous kings, such as Croesus. Under the rule of the Mermnad kings, Lydia became a massive empire that would eventually butt heads with the Persians.

The Greeks and Lydians had a peaceful relationship and shared many similarities, including religious elements and mythical figures. However, in time, the kingdom fell to Cyrus the Great and later to Alexander the Great. When the Romans emerged as a world power, Lydia was included in their empire. While the Lydians were subjected to foreign kings, they remained a unique and influential kingdom. Herodotus, the Greek historian, left behind a comprehensive report about the Lydian Empire, which has helped modern historians and archaeologists gain a better understanding of the ancient empire.

Geography

According to Herodotus, the Lydian Empire was located between the Cayster and Hermus Valleys in Anatolia. The kingdom got its name for its first king, King Lydus, and it controlled important coastal cities, such as Ephesus and Smyrna. Its geographic position allowed it to take advantage of trade and provided the Lydians with many natural resources. The land was fertile, and people had access to silver and gold from the Pactolus River. As a result of its position along trade routes and its wealth of natural resources, the kingdom became very rich. The Lydian Empire gained a reputation for being extremely wealthy, and Herodotus wrote about the empire's vast amounts of gold and silver.

At first, Lydia's neighbors included the Phrygians and Ionians, but the empire's borders exploded under the rule of the Mermnad kings, who focused much of their reigns on conquest. During its golden age, Lydian kings controlled most of Asia Minor, which was an incredible feat, and spread Lydian culture far beyond the kingdom's initial borders. However, once Lydia was conquered by the Persians and later by the Romans, the kingdom became a state, and its borders shrank again.

Sardis

The city of Sardis can be found in the modern-day province of Manisa in Turkey. It has a long and storied history since it was the capital of the Lydian Empire. When the Lydian Empire fell, the city was eventually controlled by other powers, but it still remained an influential center.

When Sardis was first built, it was simply a provincial city where the king of Lydia lived. Over time, a strict social hierarchy developed. The wealthy and elite people lived in the upper part of the city where the king resided, while the poorer members of society lived in the lower part of the city. The difference between the social classes became especially clear when archaeologists discovered that the lower part of the city wasn't protected by a wall. The poorer residents of the city lived in simple reed houses and were left vulnerable to outside invaders. Meanwhile, the upper part of the city would have been extremely luxurious, with well-built homes and temples.

According to legend, the Lydians were among the first to have permanent retail stores, which would have provided the rich residents with anything they wanted. Since Sardis was at the center of several trade routes, the wealthy residents would have had access to luxury items from all over the known world.

When the Assyrians fell in 612 BCE, Babylonia took control of most of Mesopotamia, while Lydia was left as the most powerful kingdom in Anatolia. The Lydians fostered peaceful trading relationships with most of its neighbors, and Sardis was at the center of the empire's trading system. It became an important city, as it brought people from Mesopotamia and Greece together, making it one of the most cosmopolitan cities in the world. The city was a melting pot of cultures and intellectual pursuits, which gave Sardis enduring influence. Thanks to Sardis's reputation for attracting intellectual minds, some of the most important scholars in the world were drawn to the neighboring Greek Ionian cities.

The Lydians were immensely proud of their capital city, and Herodotus wrote that King Croesus of Lydia loved showing off his hometown. However, when the Persians attacked Sardis, they were able to take control with relative ease thanks to the lack of defenses that existed in the lower city. It was only a matter of time before the Persian invaders broke through the wall that protected the upper part of the famed city.

Cyrus the Great conquered Sardis in 547 BCE, and the city was under Persian control for two hundred years. The Persians didn't change much in the city; they were probably only interested in defeating the Lydians and bringing the Ionian territories under their control. However, the Ionians rebelled against the Persians around 500 BCE, which caused the Persians to retaliate and burn down Sardis.

The city was rebuilt, and around 334 BCE, it was taken by Alexander the Great. During this time, the city experienced many changes. The old lower town was abandoned when a new section was built for poorer residents. The Temple of Artemis was built by the Greeks sometime around 300 BCE in the old lower town. A new stadium and theater were built, and a massive wall was built around the entire city.

Sardis was an important judicial city, which likely ensured its survival over the centuries. When the Romans took control of the region around 133 BCE, they made Lydia an administrative district, which increased Sardis's importance. Unfortunately, the Persians conquered the city again in 616 CE. This time, the Persians made sure to completely devastate the city so that it wouldn't be rebuilt.

While the Persians did their best to completely destroy the city, it still thrived for centuries and has been the subject of several archaeological excavations since 1958.

The Mermnad Dynasty

For centuries, the Lydian kingdom ruled fertile lands in western Anatolia and had good relationships with its neighbors. It didn't expand much during those years, but everything changed when the Mermnad dynasty began. Gyges was the first Mermnad king, but he didn't have a very good reputation, as the Greeks claimed that he was a tyrant. According to legend, Gyges was the bodyguard of King Candaules, who Gyges assassinated in order to become the next king. The Greek records state that the Oracle of Delphi praised Gyges's actions since they prevented a bloody civil war in Lydia. Gyges became the king of Lydia around 680 BCE and founded the dynasty that would lead Lydia into its golden era.

Alyattes became the king of Lydia around 610 BCE, and he set out to expand the kingdom's borders. He conquered Ionian territory and was praised for being one of the best Mermnad kings. However, it was Alyattes's son, Croesus, who would become the most famous Lydian king. Croesus became king around 560 BCE. He has been accredited with conquering all the Greek cities along the coast and stretching the kingdom's borders until Lydia and Persia were neighbors. Croesus managed to keep a good relationship with Greece and supported the Temple of Artemis at Ephesus, as well as the Oracle of Delphi.

Around that time, the Lydians became one of the first nations to mint their own coin, which helped to create the myth of Croesus's legendary wealth.

Coin Minting

Herodotus claimed that the Lydians were the first people to mint gold and silver coins. This claim is difficult to prove, but some historians agree that Lydia was the first Western nation to mint its own coins. However, the Lydians didn't use pure gold or silver but rather electrum, which is an alloy that combines gold and silver. The first Lydian coins were dated back to Alyattes I's reign (c. 610-560 BCE).

15. Lydian coin

The coins were stamped with lion head carvings, while fractions were stamped with carvings of lion paws. Later, Croesus began minting pure gold coins with a system that tested the coins' purity. This development ensured Croesus's reputation as one of the wealthiest men in the world. These coins were known as the Croeseid and came into circulation around 550 BCE. The Croeseid coins were the first bimetallic monetary system in the world. The bimetallism system refers to a system in which coins are compared to the value of certain amounts of precious metals. This would have simplified massive trade deals, which were common in Lydia, especially in Sardis. However, it took some time before the coins were used for everyday trade since they were extremely valuable. Even electrum coins were too expensive to use to pay ordinary laborers. Rather, these coins were used for massive transactions or large-scale retail purchases. Herodotus also claims that the Lydians were the first to establish permanent retail stores, which may have motivated the Lydians to develop their own coins.

In time, different types of coins were minted, including silver coins and electrum alloys that were mixed with copper. Smaller fractions were also invented, but these developments didn't impact the ordinary people, who likely would never have used these coins.

Customs and Language

Unfortunately, not much is known about Lydian customs. Historians have to rely heavily on Herodotus's account to piece together a picture of what life was like in the ancient kingdom. According to Herodotus, girls from the lower classes were forced to go into prostitution as soon as they were mature enough. They would then use the proceeds from their trade to build up a dowry. Once they had a large enough dowry, they would announce that they were available for marriage.

Unsurprisingly, the Lydians shared many customs with the Greeks, which was likely due to their close trading and commercial relationship. The Lydians were also accredited with inventing several ancient games, including knucklebones. This ancient game involved throwing several small objects into the air and collecting a certain number of throws. It has many different names and was a favorite among a number of ancient societies. Games were a way for people to escape from their ordinary lives or from stressful situations caused by droughts or other natural disasters. Herodotus also claims that the Lydians were brave and militant, which would have likely been reflected in their culture and daily lives.

The Lydians had their own language with an alphabet that shared similarities with the Greek alphabet. While historians have figured out ancient Lydian grammar, there are still some words that they don't understand. Most Lydian inscriptions are short and to the point, which makes learning the language somewhat difficult. The Lydian language has been classed as an Indo-European language, and while it shares many similarities to ancient Greek, it is still fairly unique and has several Eastern influences. Translating Lydian inscriptions has proven to be difficult, and scholars have concluded that, based on present findings, the Lydians didn't write much.

Arachne

One of the most famous myths to come from Lydia involves a skilled weaver named Arachne. There are many versions of the myth, but most versions agree that Arachne was a Lydian weaver whose father was Idmon of Colophon, a dyer of purple. In some versions, Arachne is the daughter of a shepherd. According to the myth, Arachne challenged the goddess Athena. This is a common thread in Greek mythology, and the gods never took kindly to any challenges or bragging. Arachne refused to acknowledge that her skill came from Athena and claimed that she alone was responsible for her talent.

Athena was the goddess of war, wisdom, and crafts, and Arachne's claim infuriated her. The goddess disguised herself as an old woman and warned Arachne to repent, but Arachne refused to do so. Athena then removed her disguise and responded to Arachne's challenge. They decided to participate in a weaving contest to decide whose skill was better. The goddess wove a beautiful tapestry that showed off all the gods' accomplishments. In some versions, Athena wove a tapestry that depicted what happened when mortals challenged the gods, but

Arachne created a piece that showed all the gods' failings. Her piece showed all the instances in which the gods tricked or abused humans.

When they were done, Athena inspected Arachne's work and couldn't find a single flaw. This infuriated the goddess, although Arachne's provocative depiction of the gods may also have caused the goddess to lose her temper. As a result, Athena destroyed Arachne's tapestry and hit Arachne over the head. Arachne was humiliated by Athena's actions and hung herself. However, Athena took pity on Arachne. The goddess transformed Arachne's noose into a cobweb and turned the talented weaver into a spider.

The *Metamorphoses* by Ovid, a Roman poet, is the main source of the Arachne myth and may have served as an allegory of the censorship of poetry during the reign of Roman Emperor Augustus.

Ionia

Ionia was one of the most important Greek regions. It was located on the Aegean shore in Anatolia. The Greeks set up many smaller Ionian states in Anatolia that played an important part in the classical Greek period. The "Ionian awakening" refers to a period during which Ionia played a massive role in the intellectual part of Greek society. The Greeks colonized Ionia around 1000 BCE and used Ionia's geographical position to become experienced sea traders. In time, Ionian traders became very powerful and controlled much of the political power in the states.

The Ionians also traded extensively with Egypt, Rome, and Lydia. Ionia became very wealthy thanks to its extensive trading network and had many trading colonies along the Black Sea. Ionia was mostly made up of city-states that worked together, and it controlled important ports or trading depots. Lydia and Ionia had an almost symbiotic relationship and shared many cultural traits. Thanks to the traffic that went through Sardis, the city became a hub where Mesopotamian and Greek Ionian minds met and shared ideas. This contributed greatly to Ionia's reputation as an intellectual center. However, as Sardis declined, the Ionian city of Miletus became the hub of trade and intellectuals. The knowledge that came from Sardis and Miletus was unique because scholars received information from Babylonia, Egypt, Phoenicia, and Lydia. As a result, scholars weren't overly influenced by one culture's views on religion and science. This led to advancements in the subjects of commerce, mathematics, astronomy, navigation, and geography.

The advancement of knowledge benefited both Lydia and Ionia greatly. However, the two kingdoms shared more than just a collection of scholars.

The Relationship between Lydia and Ionia

Lydia was always in contact with its neighbors, the Ionians (who were also known as the Eastern Greeks), but their relationship fluctuated according to the times. However, their relationship became steadily stronger under the Mermnad dynasty. Alyattes and Croesus managed to unite much of Asia Minor, which improved trading prospects. The Mermnad kings turned Lydia into a thriving empire that became a formidable political and economic power in Asia Minor. It would have been unwise to make an enemy out of the Lydians, so the two kingdoms opted for a peaceful relationship, which led to a mutually beneficial relationship.

Ionian and Lydian trade routes thrived thanks to this relationship, and the invention of coins made commerce much easier. The Ionians quickly adopted the practice of minting their own coins, which shows that the two kingdoms had a lot of influence on each other. The Lydians also had a similar religion to the Ionians, and Croesus famously helped build a temple to Artemis in Ionia. As the Lydian Empire rose to prominence, so did the need for luxury goods. The wealthy elite of Lydia paid handsomely for foreign and local crafts, which attracted artisans from all over the known world to Sardis and other Lydian cities. Among those were many Lydian artisans. In fact, Alyattes and Croesus employed Ionian craftsmen to create offerings to the god Apollo at Delphi. As a result, the Ionian economy benefited from Lydian wealth.

Legacy

The Mermnad kings had a great track record with the Oracle of Delphi. According to legend, the Oracle approved of Gyges's actions when he usurped the throne and allegedly guided Alyattes through a serious illness. However, that lucky streak came to an end when Croesus decided to consult the Oracle. When he asked for guidance in his war with Persia, the Oracle gave a vague reply that a kingdom would fall. Croesus took that to mean that he would win the war, but he was very wrong. In 547 BCE, Cyrus the Great conquered Sardis. The last Mermnad king was forced to retreat to his capital city, but critical weaknesses in the city's defenses meant that the city fell quickly to the Persian invaders.

When Sardis fell, so did the Lydian Empire. The Mermnad kings had turned their regional kingdom into a formidable economic, political, and cultural force, and Lydia's golden era saw great advancements in trade, knowledge, and culture. However, that wasn't enough to win the war against the Persians, who were led by one of the greatest military leaders in history.

While Lydia never recovered, it still left its mark on history. The advent of minted coins revolutionized trade in the west and was further refined by societies in the region. When Sardis fell, it left a definite hole in the intellectual world, but Miletus quickly rose as a new hub for scholars and wise men. The knowledge that had been shared at Sardis created new ways of thinking and benefited the surrounding areas for centuries. There's still a lot that historians don't know about the Lydians since they didn't leave behind many written records. However, they left behind a definite impact that was faithfully recorded by their allies and neighbors.

Chapter 5 – Classical Anatolia: Phrygia and the Phrygians

The Phrygian kingdom existed from around 1200 BCE to 700 BCE in Anatolia. When the Hittite Empire collapsed, the Phrygians came to power and created a powerful kingdom that would last for centuries. During that time, their culture included a mix of Greek, Anatolian, and Eastern elements that affected the entire region. The Phrygians were often included in Greek mythology, and their religions were very similar. Phrygia's mythology includes several famous figures, such as King Midas and Tantalus. According to Greek mythology, the Phrygians played a key part in the legendary Trojan War.

Their enduring legacy is a source of fascination to historians and archaeologists alike, as an interesting culture exists behind the various myths that sprang up around the ancient Phrygians. They were accomplished horsemen and had a complex and unique language.

Despite all the legends that exist about the Phrygians, there is still a lot that historians don't know. However, what information exists about them is enough to spark curiosity. They had an interesting history that included famous kings and mysterious organizations. The Phrygians provide a glimpse into the period between the fall of the Hittites and the rise of the Lydians, and while Phrygia never became a massive empire, it left a distinct mark on Anatolian history.

The Collapse of the Hittite Empire

Western Anatolia was a very fertile stretch of land that proved to be ideal for settlers. The Hattians made their home there around 2000 BCE, and the Hittites founded a kingdom in the region that dominated much of Anatolia. Unfortunately for the Hittites, their mighty kingdom collapsed after being attacked by the Kaskians and Assyrians. The Assyrians made sure to completely destroy the Hittite culture, which allowed other cultures to migrate into the region and make their home on the fertile plains.

Greek historians claimed that the Phrygians migrated to Anatolia from the Balkans, while some Phrygian kings allegedly had Macedonian origins. Some ancient historians connected the Phrygians to the Bryges people who originated in Europe, while some claimed that the Phrygians were linked to the Mygdones people from Macedonia. However, modern historians have dismissed many of these claims and have looked for other reasons to explain the sudden appearance of the Phrygians.

According to the Egyptians, the Hittite Empire collapsed due to repeated invasions from various Sea Peoples. Historians have theorized that the Phrygians may have been a part of these mysterious Sea Peoples who pushed their way into Hittite territory. Other theories suggest that the Phrygians migrated to Anatolia somewhere just before or after the collapse of the Hittites. One thing was for certain: when the Hittites collapsed, they left a massive power vacuum in the region that the Phrygians filled. While the Phrygians never attained the same levels of power as the Hittites, they still left a lasting influence on the region.

Rise of Phrygia

According to legend, one of the first kings of Phrygia was Gordias, who was responsible for creating the Gordian Knot. The king used the knot to fasten his cart, and an oracle prophesied that whoever was able to undo the knot would one day rule over all of Asia. The cart and knot remained at the Phrygian capital of Gordium until Alexander the Great arrived at the city. When he heard the story about the knot, he took out his sword and cut through the knot (although some versions claim that he simply removed the cart's yoke pole and slipped the knot off).

16. Alexander the Great cuts the Gordian Knot

As the Phrygian kingdom developed after the fall of the Hittite Empire, the residents benefited from the fertile lands and the trade routes that ran from Greece to Persia. Historians have found that the Phrygians were master artisans who made amazing pieces of pottery and worked with metal. They built magnificent chambered tombs for the elite members of society that displayed the wealth of the civilization. It is possible that the kingdom was enriched by fertile lands, skilled artisans, and bustling trade, which would eventually have added to the myth of the fabulously wealthy King Midas.

Historians have also found that the Phrygians were heavily influenced by the Hittite culture, and it is possible that some Hittites still remained after the Assyrians destroyed their empire. Those survivors would have been assimilated into the new powers in the region, which would have allowed elements of the Hittite culture to survive. The Phrygians also built an extensive system of roads, which would be used by other cultures after their collapse. Considering their position between the Greeks and Persians, it is unsurprising that the Phrygians were heavily influenced by those cultures.

Customs and Language

The Phrygians had their own Indo-European language, which was heavily influenced by Armenian and Greek. According to the Greek historian Herodotus, Pharoah Psamtik of Egypt wanted to determine the oldest language in the world. At that time, the Egyptians believed that they were the most ancient race, but the pharaoh wanted to prove that fact once and for all. After he tried several methods to prove his theory, he came up with an ingenious idea. He took two infants and gave them to a shepherd. The shepherd was ordered to take care of the children, but he wasn't allowed to speak to them. Once the children were old enough to speak, the pharaoh hoped that they would speak the world's first language.

When the time came, the shepherd reported to the pharaoh that the children kept repeating the word "becos." A thorough search was conducted, and it was discovered that "becos" was the Phrygian word for bread. The pharaoh was forced to admit that the Phrygians were the oldest civilization in the world.

The Phrygians were also accredited with introducing important musical techniques to the Greeks. Several Greek myths involve Phrygians in prominent roles. For example, the Greeks claimed that a Phrygian satyr (a male nature spirit with the ears and tail of a horse) named Marsyas created the aulos, which was a reed instrument. The satyr then entered a music contest against the god Apollo. When the satyr lost, Apollo flayed the musician and hung his skin on a sacred tree. Later, King Midas allegedly judged a music contest between Pan and Apollo. When the unlucky king sided with Pan, Apollo cursed the king with donkey ears.

Unfortunately, the Phrygians didn't leave behind many inscriptions, which means that historians have to rely on records left behind by other cultures. As a result, the Greeks are the main source of information about the ancient Phrygians. For example, the Phrygians are mentioned in the *Iliad*, which claims that the Phrygians were expert horsemen and produced fine wine.

Phrygian Dactyls

A mysterious class of scientists and sorcerers was known in ancient Anatolia as the Dactyls and likely originated in Phrygia. Not much is known about these sorcerers, but they had a fearsome reputation and were mentioned by several prominent ancient scholars. According to legend, the Dactyls were magicians, conjurers, soothsayers, and exorcists. They were accredited with using the Ephesian mines to discover minerals. The Dactyls also developed musical notes and brought musical instruments to Greece. The Cretans also received fire from the Dactyls.

Over time, the Dactyls were associated with divine and supernatural beings. They were accredited with discovering metallurgy, which helped to develop human society to new heights. As a result, the Dactyls took on a mythical quality. In fact, the Dactyls were a race of supernatural spirits who served the Great Mother, Cybele or Rhea. The origin of their name, which means "fingers," has been explained in several different ways. According to some sources, the name originated from the fact that they worked for the Great Mother just as fingers worked for a hand. However, others claimed that there were only ten Dactyls at a time: five men and five women. Most sources agree that the Dactyls originated in Phrygia and worshiped the goddess Rhea (or Cybele in Roman mythology).

Gordium

When the Phrygians took over, they established their capital city at Gordium. The city was placed in a prime position between Lydia and Assyria, close to the modern Sakarya River, which provided many opportunities for trade. Most Phrygian kings were buried in the city in wooden tombs that were covered by hills. These tombs have provided a wealth of information for archaeologists. One of the tombs, named Tumulus MM, may be the tomb of the legendary King Midas. It is the second-largest tomb of its kind in Anatolia. According to carbon dating, the city became important around 1000 BCE.

Gordium started off as a small town, but it quickly expanded. When it became the capital of the Phrygian kingdom, it received unprecedented influence. It was fortified and became the site of the royal palace. This would have brought the Phrygian elite to the city, who would have built fine homes there. The city was built on the ancient Persian Royal Road, which was one of the most important land routes in the region since it crossed the Sakarya River. This would have brought a lot of foreigners to the city, as well as traders and artisans. These traders would have brought treasures from all over the world to sell to the wealthy residents of the city.

Historians haven't found many Phrygian cities, which means that Phrygia likely didn't have many urban centers. However, the riches found in the tombs of the Phrygian kings hint at the idea that the Phrygians were somewhat prosperous. Historians have found many luxury items in the remains of Gordium, including Greek ceramics. Around 700 BCE, the city was sacked by the invading Cimmerians. Although the city was later rebuilt, its glory days were over. It never attained the same level of influence that it enjoyed as the capital of Phrygia.

Trojan War

The Trojan War was a conflict between the Greeks and the Trojans, who lived in Anatolia. It occurred around the 12th or 13th century. It became legendary, as it captured the imagination of the

Greeks and was immortalized in Homer's *Odyssey* and *Iliad*. The battle was also featured in Virgil's *Aeneid*. While the conflict probably wasn't as dramatic as it was portrayed in these literary works, the legend continued to grow until the battle included gods, demi-gods, and mythical heroes.

According to the *Iliad*, the Trojans had a close relationship with the Phrygians. The king of Troy, Priam, married the Phrygian princess Hecuba. Priam also supported the Phrygians when they faced off against the mythical Amazons. This would have bonded the Phrygians and Trojans. So, when it was time to go to war, the Phrygians would have fought with the Trojans.

17. Trojan horse

The Trojan War began when the prince of Troy, Paris, seduced Helen, the wife of Menelaus, King of Sparta. In retaliation, Menelaus's brother, Agamemnon, led an army against Troy. The war would last for about a decade, with heavy losses on both sides. Eventually, the Greeks built a massive wooden horse, which hid some of their best warriors inside. The Greeks then pretended to retreat and left the massive horse at the city gates. When the Trojans discovered the horse, they assumed that the Greeks had surrendered and brought the horse into their city. That night, the hidden Greek warriors slipped out of the horse, opened the gates to the waiting Greek army, and destroyed the city.

Since the account was written hundreds of years after the actual event, it's not possible to know what was true or not, but it seems very likely that the Phrygians allied with the Trojans.

King Midas

King Midas is a famous figure in Greek mythology and was known as the king of Phrygia. Historians have found inscriptions of a ruler who may have been the real-life counterpart to the myth. He was named Mita of Mushki, and he may have ruled from around 738 to 696 BCE. According to the myth, King Midas found a satyr named Silenus, who was dealing with the aftereffects of a night of heavy drinking. The king kindly returned Silenus to his master Dionysus, the god of wine. The god offered Midas a gift of his choosing, so Midas chose the ability to turn anything he touched into gold. While it was a good wish in theory, the reality turned out to be much different than what the king had imagined.

When the king tried to eat or drink, it turned to gold as soon as he touched it. The starving king begged the god to reverse the gift, and Dionysus told the king to wash off in the Pactolus River. Coincidentally, the Pactolus River in Lydia was known for its plentiful gold deposits, which later enriched the kingdom of Lydia. If Mita of Mushki was indeed the legendary king Midas, he was a wealthy mortal who allied with other rulers against King Sargon II of Assyria. However, he wasn't defeated by the Assyrians but rather the Cimmerians. One source claims that Midas died in 695 BCE; he committed suicide after he lost an important battle.

Cimmerians

The Cimmerians were a nomadic people who migrated to Anatolia around 700 BCE. They were mentioned in the *Odyssey*. According to the ancient literary work, the Cimmerians originated beyond Oceanus in a permanently dark world that served as the entrance to the underworld. However, Herodotus claims that the Cimmerians migrated from the north of the Black Sea and the Caucasus. Their society was made of a ruling elite and lower-born commoners.

Around 675 BCE, the Cimmerians entered into an alliance with the king of Urartu, Rusa II. The two nations then invaded Phrygia and destroyed the city of Gordium. According to legend, King Midas committed suicide after losing the battle. This destabilized the Phrygian kingdom, and the Cimmerians then imposed their rule on the Phrygians. The Cimmerians burned Gordium to the ground, and soon after the Phrygians were destroyed, Lydia became the dominant power in the region. According to Herodotus, the Mermnad king of Lydia, Alyattes, finally conquered the Cimmerians, after which the Cimmerians never recovered and were no longer mentioned in historical texts.

When the Cimmerians burned Gordium to the ground, they likely destroyed many important artifacts that would have shed more light on Phrygian society. Unfortunately, Phrygia was trampled by several other kingdoms, including the Lydians, destroying any lingering evidence of Phrygian society.

Lydian Conquerors

When the Cimmerians conquered Phrygia, they enjoyed control of the region for a short while but soon came into conflict with the Lydians. According to ancient accounts, the Lydians finally managed to defeat the Cimmerians around 620 BCE when the Mermnad kings decided to expand Lydia's borders and turn the kingdom into an empire. When the Cimmerians were defeated, Phrygia became a Lydian state.

Although the Lydian kings subdued Phrygia, they were still interested in maintaining the ancient kingdom. Evidence shows that King Croesus supported several building projects in Gordium in the 600s BCE. However, the Lydians didn't control all of Phrygia's old territories, as the Assyrians took over some of Phrygia's former eastern lands.

It seems that the Lydians allowed native Phrygians to continue ruling Phrygia while paying tribute to the Lydian king. According to legend, a prince of Phrygia named Adrastus accidentally killed his brother, which forced his father to exile Adrastus to Lydia. While in Lydia, he was welcomed by King Croesus, who put the Phrygian prince in charge of his own son, Atys. The pair was sent out to hunt a massive wild boar that had been terrorizing the countryside. Eventually, they spotted the beast, and Adrastus aimed his spear at the animal but accidentally hit Atys instead. The unlucky prince was forced to return to Croesus to deliver the bad news. Croesus decided to spare Adrastus since he recognized that it had been an accident. The king claimed that it was the will of the gods. However, Adrastus wasn't as kind to himself and was driven to despair. He later committed suicide in Atys's tomb.

There may be some truth in the myth, as it reflects the practice of taking royal prisoners, which would have kept the Phrygians firmly under Lydian control.

Legacy

While the Phrygian kingdom never recovered from the Cimmerian invasion, it still remained as a state. The Greeks seemed to be fond of the Phrygians, and Phrygian slaves were highly prized. This may have been due to the fact that Phrygians were highly skilled metalworkers, woodcarvers, and embroiders. Historians have uncovered the fact that Phrygians were famous for their carpets and carvings, and archaeologists have found beautifully carved shrines and tombs. It is also likely that the cult of Cybele started in Phrygia before it eventually took root in Greece.

Phrygian culture is wrapped in mystery, but historians have learned that high priests usually ruled over large portions of the land. The Phrygians were likely well-educated people who were able to read and write, and their capital city attracted artisans from Greece, Phoenicia, Syria, and Urartu. It seems that many Phrygians were experienced shepherds who worked with fine wool that they sold to many Greek cities. They also exported wool and were experienced horsemen. It's unlikely that common people rode horses, as this was likely reserved for the elite.

The Phrygians had a definite impact on the Greeks, especially since they included the Phrygians in many of their myths. While the Phrygians were brutally defeated by the Cimmerians, it is clear that they were respected by their neighbors. The Egyptians believed that the Phrygians were the oldest nation in the world, and the Greeks believed that the highly respected Dactyls originated in Phrygia. Due to their enduring impact on ancient literature, the Phrygians won't fade out of memory anytime soon.

Chapter 6 – Classical Anatolia: Urartu

The Kingdom of Urartu, also known as the Kingdom of Van, was located around Lake Van in the Armenian Highland. It rose to prominence during the Iron Age and became a wealthy nation that was known for excellent horsemanship. Urartu controlled a lot of territories in ancient Anatolia through the use of a highly trained army and several fortresses. Archaeologists have found evidence that Urartu produced amazing pieces of art, which means its population boasted mighty warriors and skilled artisans. Some of the most beautiful pieces of artwork in Anatolia were produced in Urartu, and the kingdom also had an abundance of experienced metalworkers.

Urartu had a distinct culture, and it has fascinated historians for decades, but there's still a lot that isn't known about the influential kingdom. Despite its power and accomplishments, the kingdom only lasted for about two centuries before it completely collapsed. The precise cause of the kingdom's destruction is still unknown, and most of the information about Urartu comes from ancient fragments and biased contemporary sources.

While Urartu was a relatively short-lived kingdom, it accumulated spectacular amounts of wealth and managed to pose a serious threat to the Assyrians. Urartu had no shortage of enemies and was one of the most noteworthy kingdoms in ancient Anatolia.

The Names and Origin of Urartu

Strangely enough, the name "Urartu" originated with Urartu's greatest enemy, the Assyrians. Urartu means "high place," which could possibly refer to the fact that the Urartians commonly built tall fortresses that they used to defend their territory. Urartu was also located in a rocky, mountainous region, which could also explain the name. However, the Assyrians also used the name "Urartu" to refer to the geographical region where the kingdom was based. The Babylonians referred to Urartu as "Uruartri," while the Hebrews knew Urartu as "Ararat." Some of the Urartian kings called their kingdom "Biainili or "the land of Bia." The name "Kingdom of Van" emerged as a possibility, as historians have theorized that Urartu's capital was located near Lake Van in Armenia. Some of the earliest references to the Urartians claimed that they were from the land of Nairi.

18. Urartian carving

However, it seems that Nairi was a separate and distinct area that was made up of smaller tribes and kingdoms. Assyrian King Shalmaneser I claimed to have conquered Nairi. The Assyrians repeatedly invaded the area from the reign of Shalmaneser I (around 1274 BCE) to Ashurnasirpal II (883-859 BCE). These repeated attacks would have weakened the area and made it very difficult for any independent kingdom to thrive and grow.

However, Urartu began showing up in Assyrian inscriptions around 900 BCE. It is possible that the kings of Urartu managed to unify some of the states in Nairi and create their own powerful kingdom. The Urartians would prove to be a difficult enemy for Assyria, and the two nations would be almost perpetually locked in a power struggle. Despite Assyria's large army and extensive resources, Urartu managed to hold its own for decades. Not only did it survive the Assyrians, but it also managed to thrive and become prosperous.

Rise of Urartu

While Nairi likely started off as a region full of independent states and kingdoms, it faced enough hostility from Assyria that a unified kingdom formed. It is impossible to know what happened with exact certainty, but it seems as though Urartu emerged as the ruling power in the area in the 9th century BCE. It isn't hard to see why the Assyrians would have wanted control of the region, as Urartu was well placed on fertile lands that had plenty of access to fresh water, thanks to the rivers that ran through the area. Urartian farmers grew millet, rye, sesame, barley, flax, and wheat. The area also had an abundance of fruit trees, including apples, quinces, cherries, pomegranates, and plums. The Urartians were also some of the earliest vintners in the world, as evidence of winemaking has been discovered in the area.

19. Lake Van

Farming was a lucrative practice for the Urartians, but they didn't just rely on crops. They also worked with goats, sheep, cattle, and horses. The region was well-watered and had a lot of land, which was used as pasturages for herds. Urartu also had access to gold, silver, copper, iron, tin, and lead deposits, which allowed them to become experienced metalworkers. Their metal products would become some of the most distinct pieces in Anatolian history. The Urartians had many resources and were able to trade thanks to the trade routes that ran through Anatolia, Mesopotamia, and Asia. Unfortunately, this prosperity attracted attention from other kingdoms, which then set their sights on conquering Urartu. Due to the constant need to protect themselves, the Urartians became a somewhat militant civilization.

Society and Politics

Urartu was governed by a monarchy, which was supported by a close network of administrators and councilors. Administrators were appointed to take care of the daily issues that came with ruling a kingdom and oversaw the various aspects of the government. The Urartian kings built temples, fortresses, canals, and roads that improved life for ordinary citizens and turned Urartu into a sophisticated kingdom. Historians have found evidence that Urartu's capital, Tushpa (later Van), was built in the highlands of Lake Van and may have had a population of about fifty thousand people. Many artisans and skilled workers would have lived at Tushpa, where they would have been commissioned to make luxury goods and buildings.

Tushpa was built on a mountain, which would have allowed the capital city to watch over the surrounding city. Archaeologists found the remains of royal tombs that were carved into the mountain where the capital was built. The remains of ancient Urartians have provided a lot of insight into the ancient culture. Several bodies were found in a necropolis at Çavuştepe Castle, which was part of an Urartian fortress. One of these bodies was a three-year-old who was buried with significant amounts of jewelry. Another body was buried along with jewelry and several animals.

Urartian kings spent a lot of time on military campaigns and relied on governors who acted on the king's behalf. These governors were responsible for administration, justice, and tax collection. The government was highly organized, and the Urartian kings kept control of their territory through several fortresses.

Culture

Like many of their neighbors, the Urartians were heavily influenced by other cultures. Evidence shows that Urartian culture was influenced by the Hurrians who preceded them. Since both cultures spoke similar languages, it is possible that they were connected through common ancestors. However, one of the greatest influences on Urartian culture was Assyria. The Urartian script was similar to Assyrian works. Besides their writing, the Assyrians also influenced Urartian warfare, diplomacy, and art. This likely happened when Assyria repeatedly invaded Urartu from around 1200 BCE to 800 BCE. As Urartu developed its own distinct identity, the kingdom still mimicked several Assyrian practices, which became clear as Urartu began conquering neighboring territories.

Urartu produced warriors who were known for their bravery and skill. It is clear that many Urartian kings were highly militant, and this would have been reflected in their society. However, many of the ordinary people were farmers or craftsmen. Urartu was built in a fertile region, which made farming a lucrative practice that would have supported most of the population. Religion also played a large role in Urartian society, as kings also served as priests. Urartu had a distinctive pantheon of gods, some of whom were brought over from the Hurrians, while others were uniquely Urartian. War was an important part of the Urartian culture, which is evidenced by the fact that the head of the Urartian pantheon was Haldi, the god of war. Not much is known about Haldi or his powers besides the fact that he was symbolized by a lion or bull.

Facts about the Urartian culture and their daily life have been obscured by time, but evidence of their artistic and architectural styles has been seen throughout Anatolia. Modern historians don't know as much about the ancient Urartians as they would like, but it is clear that they had a distinct impact on other Anatolian kingdoms. However, Urartu ruled over different tribes and ethnicities, which meant that the Urartians likely didn't have one united culture. It is likely that aspects of life differed depending on the region.

Language

The Urartian language went extinct centuries ago, and historians have to rely on inscriptions left by the Urartians to try and decipher it. Their language has also been referred to as Neo-Hurrian or Khaldian. The Urartian language is likely similar to the Hurrian language because the two nations probably originated from the same source. These two languages are unique, though, as scholars have failed to link them to others. The Hurro-Urartian language hasn't been linked to any other Indo-European or Semitic language, which means it stands in a class of its own.

Archaeologists have found many cuneiform inscriptions in Urartu that were written in the Urartian language but used the Assyrian script. Some inscriptions were written in Akkadian, which was used in Assyria. This helped to translate the inscriptions. It seems that the Urartians developed their own system of hieroglyphs that predated the

Assyrian cuneiform script. These hieroglyphs eventually faded from common use and seemed to have been used only by priests and administrators between the 9th to the 6th centuries BCE. Historians haven't been able to decipher most of these hieroglyphs, which makes it difficult to know what they represented. In fact, some scholars don't believe that the hieroglyphs were used for writing.

Unfortunately, the true nature of the Urartian language might never be known since little remains of the dead language.

Urartu's Kings

The first recorded Urartian king was Arame, who reigned from about 860 to 840 BCE. His successor, Sarduri I, who reigned from about 835 to 825 BCE, helped raise Urartu into a unified kingdom that eventually posed a serious threat to the Assyrians. While the Assyrians were a major power in the region, they fell into a dark age around 800 BCE, which would have prevented them from launching any serious military attacks on Urartu. This dark age lasted for a few decades, and it was during this time that Urartu grew powerful.

Sarduri I was able to fend off attacks from Assyrian King Shalmaneser III and worked on strengthening Urartu's military and the monarchy's power. He made Tushpa the Urartian capital, and his son, Ishpuini, elevated Haldi to the head of the Urartian pantheon. Ishpuini is also known as the first Urartian king to write his inscriptions in the Urartian languages; previous kings had used the Akkadian language. This might mean that Urartu had a distinctive culture and language, allowing the Urartians to move further away from Assyrian influence.

Ishpuini conquered Musasir (a neighboring society) and fended off an attack from Assyrian King Shamshi-Adad V. For some reason, he appointed a man named Menua as his vice-regent, and the two men ruled jointly until Ishpuini died. While Menua also expanded Urartu, his son, Argishti I, conquered more territory. Argishti I conquered many of Urartu's neighbors and built several cities and fortresses, which helped him control his newly acquired lands. He reigned from about 785 to 760 BCE and managed to prevent Assyrian King Shalmaneser IV from invading the region.

There were several other notable Urartian kings, including Rusa I. Unfortunately, Urartu would face more serious threats from Assyria.

Urartian Warfare

Warfare was a massive part of life in Urartu, as is evidenced by the fact that almost all the Urartian kings went to war as soon as they could. This would have had a definite impact on the ordinary citizens of the kingdom, who would have had to provide for the king and his army. Keeping an army is an expensive exercise, and it seemed as though the Urartians were perpetually engaged in war. Men would have been drafted into the army, and a lot of the country's resources would have been dedicated to supporting and feeding the soldiers. At first, the Urartians were forced to engage in warfare since the Assyrians persistently invaded the territory. However, once the Assyrians declined somewhat, the Urartians seemed to have learned from the Assyrians and turned their sights on conquering their neighbors.

Archaeologists have found weapons that were dedicated at several temples, which have provided an insight into the Urartian army. These weapons included swords, javelins, bows, and spears. Soldiers wore helmets and metal armor and carried heavy shields engraved with animals such as bulls and lions. It's likely that ordinary soldiers weren't as well protected, but the elite carried impressive weapons, armor, and shields. The Urartians were renowned for their horse rearing, which means that they likely used cavalries and chariots in their battles. Since the Urartian army was heavily influenced by the Assyrians, who used horses extensively, it isn't unreasonable to assume that the Urartian army used horses as well.

Urartu was a powerful and militant kingdom, which meant they had several enemies. The kingdom certainly benefited from the Assyrian Empire's slump in the 800s BCE, but unfortunately, that slump came to an end, and Assyria once again set its sights on Urartu.

The only difference was that future Assyrian kings were much more aggressive and determined.

Urartu vs. Assyria

The Urartians had been defeated by the Assyrians on several occasions but always managed to regroup and rebuild. They became wealthy from trade and their abundant resources, which allowed them to equip their army with some of the best weapons in the world at that time. They also raised horses and trained them specifically for war. When Sargon II of Assyria inherited the throne around 722 BCE, the Urartians posed a serious threat to Assyria. He launched a few campaigns against the kingdom during his early reign, but they were all defeated. It became clear that he needed a decisive victory.

Urartu was very well defended, and due to the rocky geographical location, Urartian warriors would simply slip away into the landscape when they were in danger. This made it extremely difficult to completely destroy the Urartians. Sargon II decided to invade Urartu in 714 BCE but had to devise a new way to attack the kingdom. He slipped around to the east of Urartu, hoping to catch the Urartian army off guard. Unfortunately, it was an extremely difficult endeavor, and by the time the two armies met, the Assyrian army was severely demoralized and refused to fight. The Assyrians were unfamiliar with the mountainous region and were used to fighting on flat landscapes.

Sargon II was forced to lead the charge himself, and he risked his life in the process. His desperate decision worked, and his army rallied around him. The Urartian army was overwhelmed and forced to retreat. Sargon II chose not to pursue his enemies but looted the Urartian holy city of Musasir. According to legend, Urartu's king, Rusa I, committed suicide after the defeat.

The Fall of Urartu

During its history, Urartu became an incredibly wealthy kingdom. In fact, when Sargon II sacked Musasir, his army carried away tons of gold, precious gems, and silver. However, the kingdom began to decline between 640 and 590 BCE. The reasons for this decline aren't certain. Many Urartian cities were completely destroyed during this time. It is possible that they faced attacks from foreign invaders such as the Scythians and Cimmerians, but the empire may have been torn apart by rebellious states. Besides the mysterious threat that took out several Urartian cities, the empire had already been weakened by near-constant attacks from Assyria. It also seems that the Urartian kings had begun having difficulty controlling their kingdom, which may support the idea that Urartu faced trouble within its borders.

Historians have also suggested that several cities were destroyed at different times and may not have been destroyed in one go. The site of Teishebaini suggests that the people were caught by surprise since valuable belongings were abandoned and the city's granaries were still full. Arrowheads found at the site were similar to those used by the Scythians, so it is possible that the Scythians may have attacked the city. Urartu gradually weakened over a few decades, so when the Medes marched against the kingdom around 585 BCE, Urartu finally fell. It was incorporated into Cyrus the Great's territories.

Legacy

Urartu was one of the greatest classical Anatolian empires. Its people were fierce warriors who baffled the Assyrian army with their ability to escape into the landscape. They were also skilled horsemen whose abilities were famous. While much of their culture is shrouded in mystery, it is clear that they were farmers, vintners, herdsmen, horsemen, and artisans. Their origins and language aren't precisely known, but after surviving numerous attacks from the Assyrians, they were able to become a distinct culture that bore some foreign influences. Their art and architecture survived the destruction of their civilization.

The Greeks were largely unaware of Urartu, which meant that Greek historians didn't write about the ancient culture. For centuries, Urartu lay forgotten beneath the earth until archaeologists stumbled across the ancient sites in the 19th century CE. The discovery of Urartu was a fantastic find, and it shed a lot of light on ancient Anatolian history. For centuries, the history of the region had been completely lost, but when archaeologists brought the ancient civilization to light, it bolstered Armenian nationalism. There's still a lot that archaeologists need to discover, but it is possible that more information about the ancient kingdom will come to light.

Urartu grew into an impressive kingdom when individual tribes and states were united under one monarch. This allowed the Urartians to make the best use of their abundant resources. It is possible that many of these tribes retained their own cultures, which would have made the Urartian population quite diverse. Their artisans also created works that would influence other cultures in the region and leave behind clues about the great civilization that once existed around Lake Van.

Chapter 7 – Anatolian Art, Architecture, and Archaeology

Ancient Anatolian civilizations may be shrouded in mystery and provide archaeologists with few answers, but what they lack in information, they make up for with art. There are several informative archaeological sites in modern-day Turkey that have provided scholars with a wealth of artifacts that attest to the skill of ancient Anatolian artisans. Each city and settlement enrapture archaeologists with their architecture and intricate pieces of art. Each ancient culture was unique but bore the influences of its neighbors or predecessors. While these cultures failed to leave behind precise written documents, a lot can be learned from the way they constructed buildings or the artifacts that they crafted.

Starting from Hattian pieces left behind at several archaeological sites to Lydian artifacts that bear Phrygian, Greek, and Ionian influences, this chapter delves into the complexity of the ancient Anatolian art world. While ancient Anatolia's history is fascinating, the journey to understanding that history is also noteworthy. For decades, archaeologists have made astounding finds in modern-day Turkey, but early archaeologists also made mistakes and great claims that impacted Anatolian archaeology for years. Many of these cultures went extinct centuries ago, but their art and architecture remain, allowing archaeologists to decode their stories.

Priam's Treasure

The story of the Trojan War and Homer's works have become legendary and captured the public's imagination ever since the stories were first told. They had such a firm grasp on people that early archaeologists set out to find which parts of the legend were founded in reality. In the 1800s CE, Frank Calvert and Heinrich Schliemann uncovered a veritable treasure trove at Hissarlik in modern Turkey at a site they were convinced was ancient Troy. As a result, they claimed that the treasure belonged to King Priam from Homer's epic.

In 1822 CE, Hissarlik was identified as the possible site of ancient Troy. In the 1870s, Schliemann began working on the site. He had no doubt that he had found Troy, and it became widely accepted. Together, Calvert and Schliemann found various artifacts, including golden jewelry, belts, brooches, and buttons, all of which Schliemann attributed to King Priam. The treasure trove also included shields, golden bottles, electrum cups, and weapons. It was a magnificent find that would have excited anyone.

20. Priam's treasure

Schliemann smuggled much of the treasure out of the country and lost his right to excavate at the site. Later, he bribed Ottoman officials using the treasure. Much of the treasured ended up at the Royal Museums of Berlin but were smuggled to Moscow after the Battle of Berlin. The Trojan treasure is now housed at the Pushkin Museum in Russia.

There have been doubts about the treasure trove's authenticity since Schliemann didn't have the most trustworthy reputation, but the pieces are undoubtedly beautiful. Schliemann claimed to have smuggled the treasure away from the site using his wife's shawl but later recanted his story since his wife was attending a funeral at the time of the discovery. While Schliemann thought the treasure belonged to King Priam, it is possible that the artifacts predate King Priam by a few centuries. Later, Carl Blegen confirmed that Hissarlik was the site of ancient Troy and oversaw excavations at the site on behalf of the University of Cincinnati.

Alaca Hüyük

The Hittite period produced some of the finest art in ancient Anatolia. The capital city of Hattusa was built along a gorge, with the citadel built on the highest point. Over time, the city became the capital of an empire, and Hattusa expanded along with the Hittites' status. This expansion also involved fortifications that would have protected the city from potential invaders. The city had double walls with towers built into them that allowed soldiers to patrol the walls and keep watch for any enemies. Hattusa was a magnificent city with palaces, temples, and large residential homes. The Hittite temples were massive complexes with pillar colonnades, storerooms, shrines, statues, and stone reliefs. Hittite temples were unique and vastly different from temples found in Mesopotamia. The Hittites also carved statues representing sphinxes or lions that guarded their gateways.

21. Alaca Hüyük sphinx gate

One of the most famous examples can be found at the site of Alaca Hüyük, which features a sphinx gate that leads to a big Hittite building. Excavation at the site started as early as 1907 CE. While it was thought that the site belonged to simple farmers, a large necropolis was discovered there. The people were buried with pieces of pottery, jewelry, and gold chalices. Historians also found carvings of female idols, which likely represented a mother goddess. These items made it clear that the people of Alaca Hüyük were accomplished and refined.

Beycesultan

The site of Beycesultan in western Anatolia can be found a few miles away from the modern city of Çivril in Turkey. It is a remarkable site, but due to the lack of written records found there, not much is known about its history or inhabitants. Historians have found evidence that the city was occupied in the Late Chalcolithic period. During the Bronze Age, it reached prominence, and it bears strong Aegean and Cretan influences. During this period, a palace and religious and administrative buildings were constructed. However, around 1700 BCE, the palace was destroyed, and the city was slowly abandoned.

When the Hittites emerged as the ruling power in the region, the city was slowly reinhabited while gaining strong Hittite influences. It is clear that the city never again reached the same heights that it once occupied, but it still grew substantially. Unfortunately, it was completely destroyed sometime in the 1200s BCE. Over time, the city was sporadically inhabited and became a town during the Byzantine era.

22. Beycesultan

Excavations at the site began in the 1950s. The site consists of two mounds that are separated by an old road. James Mellaart, an English archaeologist, discovered "champagne-glass" style pottery from the Bronze Age. The architecture of the site is just as astounding. Archaeologists have found houses, a palace, and a Bronze Age public house (a bar or tavern). The palace was built with a washroom at the entrance, which evidently meant that visitors had to wash before entering. The palace's interior had raised floors, which may have been part of a heating system; this would have put the palace centuries ahead of its time. The site also had a row of shops, and the tavern had a massive supply of glasses, which they would have used to serve guests.

Horoztepe and Mahmatlar

Horoztepe and Mahmatlar are two important archaeological sites that have yielded incredible finds that can be linked back to the Hattian civilization. Horoztepe was built overlooking a fertile valley, and archaeologists have found prehistoric artifacts, such as flint tools, hand mills, and potsherds, there. They also found several burial sites, which could provide a clearer understanding of ancient Anatolian burial customs. Several metal objects were also found, including bull figurines, a sun-standard, daggers, and spearheads.

Many of the objects found at Horoztepe and Mahmatlar are distinctly different from the objects found at Alaca Hüyük, which is noteworthy since the sites share a few similarities. For example, a stag figurine found at Horoztepe was made with a long body, a short tail, thick legs, and antlers. The eye sockets were made with a sharp object that pierced the figurine from both sides, which is a technique that wasn't used on any figurines at Alaca Hüyük. It would appear as though many of the artifacts at Alaca Hüyük were collected as gifts to bury with the dead, but the objects at Horoztepe don't seem to have served that purpose.

23 Figurine found at Horoztepe

Several axes were found at Mahmatlar and other Anatolian sites, but the ones found at Horoztepe are unlike any other axes found in Anatolia. The ax from Horoztepe is thin and long. It resembles a hammer, with a long sharp point on the other end. These types of artifacts raise more questions than answers, and they make Horoztepe and Mahmatlar fascinating sites that will continue to be excavated for years to come.

Hittite Art

The Hittites were a highly influential culture that controlled all of Asia Minor at the height of their power. Historians have pinpointed the height of their artistry to the period between 1450 and 1200 BCE.

It seems that Hittite art was heavily influenced by Sumerians and Babylonians but developed into a unique style that is still recognizable today. Early Hittite sites have yielded intricate bronze and gold pieces that show the skill of Hittite artisans, who would have had access to some of the finest materials in the empire and been encouraged to advance their skills. These pieces would have been traded throughout Anatolia, and they would have been prized pieces in the homes of the social elite.

As the Hittites rose in power, they began dominating their neighbors. This domination meant that several cultures were adopted into theirs. These cultures didn't simply go extinct; rather, facets of these cultures were incorporated into the Hittite culture. For example, as the Hittites rose in power, they came to worship many Mesopotamian gods, which were then added to the Hittite pantheon. Hittite artisans felt moved to sculpt idols and figurines that represented these new gods. Male figurines usually had short robes, pointed hats, and curled-toe boots, while females had square headdresses and long robes. While the Hittites carved animal figurines, they were mostly focused on religious figurines with human aspects.

A shrine found at Yazilikaya (located near the ancient city of Hattusa) has numerous rock reliefs carved by the Hittites. These reliefs portrayed gods and goddesses who were accompanied by lions and sphinxes. While other works depict humans (sometimes Hittite kings or officials) worshiping various gods or goddesses, these pieces may have been created to seek favor with the gods or to appease the deities.

24. Hittite figurine of a priest, king, or deity

Many of the reliefs involve symbolism, which provides insight into the Hittite religion. For example, one depiction of the god Tarhun has the god holding grapes and grain, which likely symbolizes the god's fertility. The Hittites were known for being master metalworkers who created beautiful carvings. Some carvings feature gold and precious stones, such as lapis lazuli, which make the carvings all the more impressive.

At some point in their history, the Hittites began using Babylonian cuneiform, which was then included in the inscriptions they added to their monuments. Besides cuneiform, they also used a hieroglyphic system that was included in inscriptions as well. Given their carving skill, it makes sense that the Hittites would have enjoyed working with hieroglyphs. The Hittites also produced beautiful pieces of pottery, including vases that were shaped to represent animals or other items, such as boots. These vases were then painted with patterns or with depictions of impressive scenes, such as marriages.

When the Hittites rose to power, many neighboring powers used cylinder seals. These seals were used to identify people and sign contracts; in fact, they were so important in certain ancient cultures that they can be compared to modern-day credit cards. However, the Hittites developed signet seals, which contained cuneiform and certain figures. These were used to identify people and or in business deals. These pieces were less magnificent than Hittite pottery or carvings, but they played an important role in everyday life.

Urartu Period

The Urartians were a somewhat militant civilization that ruled much of the region that now makes up modern-day Armenia. However, they also developed extraordinary pieces of art that still cause people to flock to see their displays in modern museums. The Urartians are known for their bronze figurines and paintings. Like the Hittites, the Urartians adopted cultural styles from the people they conquered, but the Urartian artisans also possessed incredible skills, which allowed them to expertly incorporate different cultural styles into their works.

Unfortunately, Urartu was dominated by Assyria, and much of its art was lost due to plundering and the ravages of time. This makes it difficult for historians to pinpoint exact periods in Urartu's long history. The artworks that remain have been carefully studied and can be found in museums across the world. Historians have also found that it's better to study the artworks from Urartu without comparing them to other cultures, as it is almost impossible to find the links between them. As a result, Urartu became known for its metalworkers and wall painters. It seems that Urartu's artisans had a soft spot for cauldrons, which were made from different types of metal.

As historians dig into Urartu's past and more artifacts are discovered, it is clear that the Urartians got inspiration from the Hittites, Hurrians, Egyptians, and Assyrians. Many Urartian pieces have been found at Assyrian sites, which means that either Assyria looted a lot of Urartian art or Urartian artisans traded with Assyria. It's possible that Assyria traded with Urartu but also plundered Urartian cities during their numerous invasions. However, pieces found at Urartian sites have less Assyrian influences. Urartian artisans likely developed their skills over the centuries.

Urartu's artists worked with various metals, including tin, iron, bronze, copper, silver, and gold, as well as alloys like electrum and brass. Urartians made pottery, figurines, armor, paintings, and furniture. They also engraved their weapons. Besides metal, artists also used animal bones, horns, enamel, precious stones, ivory, and enamel. It's known that the Urartians carved massive sculptures, but so far, none of these sculptures have been found intact. Instead, archaeologists have to piece together fragments since most of these sculptures were destroyed. However, reconstructions of these sculptures can be found at museums, which provide a glimpse of the Urartian artisans' skills. Most large-scale sculptures seem to depict gods or rulers.

Some of the most famous pieces from Urartu are metal cauldrons, which feature animal heads as handles. The craftsmen seemed to have preferred working with bronze and copper. Some cauldrons stand on bases or legs and are rounded at the base. Many of the cauldrons depict winged goddesses, which may be the goddess Tushpuea, who was associated with the sun god. These cauldrons are similar to Etruscan pieces. The Etruscan civilization inhabited central Italy between the 8th and 3rd centuries BCE. It is possible that the Etruscans were influenced by the Urartians or even got a hold of Urartian cauldrons. Besides cauldrons, the Urartians also made bells, amulets, seals, jewelry, figurines, candelabra, and belts.

25. Urartian bull head

The Urartians also crafted intricate pieces of pottery and painted interior walls with pictures of mythical creatures, religious figures, and ordinary scenes, such as hunting and farming. Urartian furniture was also beautifully designed and would have graced the homes of royals and the social elite.

The Phrygian Period

The Urartians and Phrygians had something in common: they both had an impact on Etruscan art. It would seem that the Phrygians also had dealings with the Urartians since archaeologists found a Phrygian cauldron bearing an Urartian bull figure. Apparently, the Phrygian artisans imported bull figurines, which they then added to their own works. The Phrygians worked with metal, pottery, and jewelry, and they were mostly influenced by Urartu and Assyria.

Phrygian pottery was incredibly fine, and pottery from different periods bears influences from different cultures. For example, earlier pottery bears distinct Lydian artistic styles, while later pottery bears

Hittite themes and motifs. Decorations on the pottery range from simple geometric patterns to complicated, colorful decorations. It would seem that many of these pieces weren't used in everyday life but were reserved for funerary gifts, which explains why they were so well preserved. A popular exhibit can be found at the Anatolian Civilizations Museum in Ankara, Turkey.

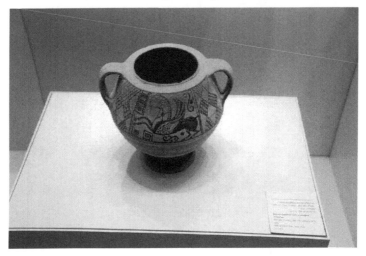

26. Phrygian clay pot

Archaeologists also found Tumulus MM at the site of Gordium, which is thought to be the tomb of the legendary King Midas. The funerary monument is large and was evidently built for a very important man. Inside, they found a wooden structure that housed a body dressed in royal garments. The monument contained evidence of the man's last meal or a feast that was laid out within the tomb. Certainly, ancient Phrygian art and architecture still have a lot to teach historians.

Lydian Treasure

Lydia was an incredibly powerful and wealthy kingdom that reached its peak under the legendary King Croesus. This prosperity allowed Lydians to decorate their homes with luxury items and commission lavish pieces that were used as decoration, jewelry, or funerary gifts. As the Lydians went on to conquer more territories, their art and architecture were influenced by the cultures that they assimilated. However, the same happened when Lydia was conquered by foreign powers, and Lydian art came to incorporate the styles and motifs of their conquerors.

27. Lydian gold figurine

Since wealthy Lydians were buried with incredible riches, their graves and tombs provide historians with valuable artifacts that can be used to study Lydian culture. Unfortunately, these graves became the target of thieves, who plundered the burial sites and smuggled their newfound treasures out of Turkey. They were then sold across the world. These treasures eventually found their way into various museums, but after lengthy battles, many pieces were returned to Turkey, where they were placed in the care of Ankara's Museum of Anatolian Civilizations.

Lydian artwork consists of metal vessels, jewelry, tools, figurines, wall paintings, and bowls. Each of these pieces was expertly crafted and lovingly buried with ancient Lydians. The plundering of Lydian burial mounds resulted in the untold loss of archaeological evidence, which would have provided amazing insight into the Lydian culture. The loss of these precious resources has drawn attention from the international scholarly community, and there have been calls for stricter laws regarding archaeological excavations. While Anatolia still has many treasures to offer, the plundering of ancient graves has left gaping holes in the historical record.

Ancient Anatolia's history may not have been written down precisely, but the artworks left behind by these ancient cultures tell the story of resilience, development, and interactions with other great nations. These factors provide historians with invaluable information about what life was like in ancient Anatolia.

Chapter 8 – Mythology and Religion

Ancient Turkish history is filled to the brim with interesting stories and myths. Each culture that rose to prominence had its own religion and set of gods, which reflected the people's way of thinking. These gods took on a life of their own as their cults devised elaborate ways to honor the deities. Artworks, buildings, and traditions were created around each culture's pantheon of gods and goddesses. This led to many interesting myths and stories that can still be shared today. The stories that are still around would have been heard and spread by ancient people who had no other way to leave their mark on the world around them.

Some of these gods and religions were so influential that other cultures adopted them and added them to their own pantheon. For example, many of the Greek gods were either influenced by Anatolian gods or may even have originated in Anatolia. Many Greek myths, such as the ones involving Midas, Tantalus, Arachne, Omphale, and others, featured Anatolian characters. Besides those famous examples, there are also myths that belong exclusively to Anatolia and its distinct cultures. These religions and deities represented entire cultures. At one point, they were the recipients of religious devotion, but now they are mere echoes of cultures that went vanished centuries ago.

The Hittite Pantheon

The Hittite religion revolved around making sure that their local god or goddess was happy and pleased with their people. The most commonly worshiped gods were a god of fertility that also managed the weather and a mother goddess. The chief god of the Hittite pantheon seemed to be the fertility/weather god. This god was usually presented as having a wife and children. He was known as Tarhun to the Hittites, Taru to the Hattians, and Teshub to the Hurrians. Not only did Tarhun control fertility and the weather, but he also granted ruling powers to kings and determined the victory of warring armies. He was commonly represented by a bull.

28. Hittite storm god

Tarhun's consort was the sun goddess Arinnitti, who is thought to be the patron goddess of the lost city of Arinna. It's possible that she was associated with the underworld or may have had some darker aspects. The king and queen of the Hittites were also considered the chief priest and priestess of Tarhun's and Arinnitti's cults. The king would have to travel within his kingdom to oversee important festivals and religious occasions in order to represent the great god.

Tarhun and Arinnitti had a son named Nerik, who was also a weather god. They had two daughters named Mezzulla and Hulla. Besides Arinnitti, there was a sun god named Istanu. He was the sun god of the water, which may refer to the sun's reflection in the water, but it is clear that he and Arinnitti had separate cults. The Hittites also had a moon god and a hunting god, as well as a goddess who represented love and war named Shaushka, who bore many similarities to the Babylonian goddess Ishtar. There were many other gods and goddesses as well, such as the mother goddess Hannahanna.

The Hittites worshiped spirits of mountains and rivers, as well as past kings and queens. Another important mythological figure was Telepenus, who featured prominently in several Hittite myths.

The Myth of Telepenus

Telepenus (also spelled Telepinus or Telepinu) was a Hittite god who was likely a farming or storm god. In some variations of the myth, he appears to be the son of Tarhun or Tessub and Arinnitti. Some sources link him to the goddess Hatepuna, but others say he had other wives. Every nine years, a festival was held in his honor, and hundreds of animals were sacrificed to him. He was represented by an oak tree, which was ceremonially planted at every festival. It would appear as though he was responsible for crops and a good harvest, which would have been an important part of life in the Hittite Empire.

However, according to a famous myth, Telepenus disappeared suddenly, which caused the harvest to fail. Naturally, this caused a disaster in the empire, and the other gods were forced to search for him. In an effort to bring Telepenus back, Hannahanna, the mother goddess, came up with an ingenious plan. She sent a bee to find the errant god. When the bee found the god, it stung Telepenus, which caused the god to fly into a rage. Telepenus then went on a rampage and caused much destruction. The goddess of magic intervened by sending Telepenus's anger to the underworld, which calmed the god down. However, there are several variations of the myth in which Telepenus's anger was sent to the underworld by a priest who earnestly prayed on behalf of the people on earth. Telepenus, or Telepinus, had a lasting effect on Hittite mythology, and several kings used his name as their own.

Lydian Pantheon

The Lydian religion was comprised of several Greek and Anatolian gods. The Lydians worshiped the mother goddess, Cybele, as did other Anatolian civilizations. Cybele was often represented by lions, which can be seen in much of her iconography. Another goddess was Artemis, which the Lydians shared with the Greeks. Notably, King Croesus made generous donations to the construction of her temple at Ephesus, and one of her sanctuaries was located near Sardis and the tombs of the Lydian kings. The Lydians also had a cult to Kore, the maiden goddess who was associated with spring. Her form appeared on several coins from Lydian cities, and she continued to be worshiped in the region when she became Persephone.

The Lydian kings also gave honor to several Greek gods, including Zeus and Apollo. In fact, the Lydian kings were famously fond of visiting Apollo's sanctuary at Delphi, where they consulted the Oracle and made substantial offerings to the god. Other deities worshiped by the Lydians include Dionysus and Hermes. The Lydian religion included altars, sanctuaries, and rituals. They used to leave animal sacrifices at the altars of their god to either appease or please the deities.

It's not surprising that Lydia shared many deities with the Greeks considering their close ties. Their religion also impacted their art since they fashioned figurines representing their gods. They also carved scenes featuring gods and goddesses into their walls. When King Croesus famously donated resources to the construction of Artemis's temple, he managed to display his piety and wealth to the world.

Urartian Pantheon

The Urartian religion was heavily impacted by Hurrian and Mesopotamian influences. According to an inscription found near the ancient capital, there were seventy-nine gods who all required different sacrifices and rituals. It's possible that the pantheon expanded to include local gods, and ancient animistic beliefs were incorporated into the culture as the Urartians conquered more territory. The religion had a divine trinity at the top headed by the gods Haldi, Shivini, and Teisheba. The head of the gods was Haldi, who was the god of war, and his consort was Arubani. Teisheba, who was a weather god known for controlling storms, was married to the goddess Huba. Shivini was the sun god, and he was married to the goddess Tushpuea. Most settlements were given their own gods, and the gods were often named after the sites they presided over. For example, the capital of Tushpa was named after Tushpuea.

Haldi was promoted to his position as the head of gods by King Ishpuini, and all wars were sanctioned by him. He was a foreign god who was adopted by the Urartians, and his role in Urartians society, besides warfare, is unknown. All kings had to seek his favor before going to war, and they were required to leave behind a record of events for the god to review when the war was over. Haldi was extremely important to the Urartians. The king of Urartu was even known as "a servant of Haldi." During times of peace, kings dedicated many construction projects to their principal god. Temples were an important part of Urartian society and had their own lands that contributed to the economy.

Phrygian Religion

Like the Lydian religion, the Phrygians worshiped a mixture of Anatolian, local, and Greek gods. It is clear that the Phrygians and Greeks had close religious ties since the Phrygians are frequently featured in famous Greek myths, such as the myth of Tantalus, the Trojan War, and the myth of King Midas. The Phrygians worshiped the god Men (an Anatolian moon god), Zeus, Apollo, and a few obscure deities who were only referred to as "holy and just." There were also several important mother goddesses who were also worshiped, including Cybele.

Cybele was widely worshiped in Asia Minor, and she was known for being a mother goddess. She was also closely associated with the god Attis, who the Phrygians believed was the god of vegetation. According to mythology, Attis and Cybele were lovers until Attis chose to marry a mortal woman. Cybele flew into a jealous rage and caused the wedding guests to fall into a state of panic. Attis was overwhelmed and distraught, and he fled into the wild. There, he descended into madness. While in this state, he castrated himself and then committed suicide.

Cybele regretted what she had done and begged Zeus to preserve Attis's body. As a result, Attis would return to life every year as vegetation once the winter months had ended. The worship of Cybele continued after the Romans took over the Greek pantheon. The Cybelean festival was a popular celebration that was held in the spring.

29. Cybele

Most Phrygian gods had their own cults, which were responsible for worshiping and appeasing their god. Phrygian gods seemed to have exemplified the characteristics of vengeance, justice, and righteousness.

Tantalus

Tantalus was a mythological figure who was sometimes referred to as the king of Phrygia. However, some sources claim that he was the king of Sipylus, which was situated between Phrygia and Lydia. He was known for his vast wealth and for being the son of Zeus and Pluto, a nymph. He was also the father of Niobe, who was punished by the gods as well. Apparently, Niobe bragged about the fact that she was superior to the goddess Leto because she had more children. Leto responded by having her children, Artemis and Apollo, kill Niobe's children. Tantalus's son was named Pelops; he was known as a hero of Olympia, which was a sanctuary dedicated to Zeus.

However, Tantalus is most known for his disastrous interaction with the gods and a particularly cruel punishment.

There are several different versions of his myth. All sources agree that Tantalus was invited with a few other mortals to attend a dinner with the gods on Mount Olympus, the home of the gods. However, after this important event, the sources begin to differ. According to some sources, Tantalus gossiped about the gods to other humans, while other sources state that he stole ambrosia, the food of the gods, and distributed it to other mortals. The most famous version of the myth is much gorier. Apparently, Tantalus decided to test the gods. He murdered his son Pelops and then cut him up and cooked him to serve to the gods. Most of the Olympians knew right away that something was wrong, but Demeter, who was suffering the loss of her daughter, accidentally took a bite of Pelops's shoulder.

The gods were disgusted by Tantalus's actions, and Zeus came up with an ingenious punishment. The gods put Pelops back together (but had to give him a prosthetic shoulder) and resurrected him. Zeus then cursed Tantalus. Once Tantalus arrived in the afterworld, he suffered terrible hunger and thirst. The king was then made to stand in a pool of refreshing water, but every time he reached for it, the water would rush away from him. He was also forced to stand beneath a fruit tree bearing ripe, juicy fruit, but every time he reached for a piece, it would be yanked away from his grasp. As a result of his treachery, Tantalus was made to keep reaching for what he could never get a hold of but desperately needed.

Midas

In Greek mythology, King Midas is known as the greedy king who received a gift from Dionysus in return for caring for one of the god's satyrs. Midas asked for the gift of turning anything he touched into gold. It was granted to him, but the king quickly realized his mistake when he tried to eat food, as it turned to gold in his hands. He had to petition the god to remove the gift, and Dionysus commanded the king to wash in the Pactolus River.

King Midas was also involved in another unfortunate myth. According to this myth, King Midas judged a competition of skill between Pan and Apollo. Both were musical gods, and they wanted to test who had the best skills. Pan was responsible for creating the panpipes, while Apollo occupied a more important position as the god of music.

King Midas declared Pan the winner, which infuriated Apollo. He cursed King Midas, leaving him with donkey ears. Midas was forced to wear a hat to hide his deformity, but he needed someone to cut his hair. He forced his barber to swear that he would never reveal his secret. This proved to be too difficult for the barber. In an effort to get rid of the need to tell anyone, the barber dug a hole next to a river and whispered the king's secret into the ground before covering it up again.

30. King Midas with donkey ears

Reeds grew from the spot where the barber had whispered the words, and when the wind blew through them, the reeds sang out the secret. Soon, the whole kingdom knew that Midas had donkey ears, which caused the king to execute his barber before committing suicide.

The Slaying of the Dragon

In Hittite mythology, a popular myth exists involving the god Tarhun and a fearsome dragon named Illuyanka. There are several versions of the myth. According to one source, Tarhun and Illuyanka fought each other, and Illuyanka won. The dragon then took the god's heart and eyes. The defeated god retreated and married a poor woman, who gave birth to a son that eventually married Illuyanka's daughter. Before the wedding, Tarhun's son approached Illuyanka and asked for his father's eyes and heart as a gift. Illuyanka relented. As soon as Tarhun had his heart and eyes, he returned to Illuyanka, and they resumed their fight. However, just as Tarhun was about to kill Illuyanka, the storm god's son discovered that he had been used by his father to trick his mother-in-law. The son was horrified and demanded that Tarhun kill him, along with Illuyanka. Tarhun obliged and killed his son and the dragon.

In another version, after Tarhun lost the battle, he approached the goddess Inara for advice. Inara turned to a mortal named Hupasiyas for help. Together, they invited the dragon to a feast, where the dragon was given large amounts of food and drink. When the dragon fell asleep, Hupasiyas tied the dragon up with rope. Tarhun was then able to kill the dragon without any trouble.

Omphale and Heracles

In Greek and Roman mythology, the hero Heracles (or Hercules) was forced to serve the queen of Lydia, Omphale, for three years after killing Iphitos, the son of Eurytus. Omphale's kingdom was overrun by monsters and bandits, so she instructed the hero to free her land from these pests. Heracles was able to free Omphale's kingdom, which caused her to fall in love with him. In time, the two became lovers. At some point in their relationship, Omphale forced Heracles to wear women's clothing while she wore men's clothing. She also made him do demeaning womanly chores. This reversal in gender roles was likely played for laughs among Greek audiences. During his time in Lydia, Heracles buried Icarus and took part in Jason and the Argonauts' quest to retrieve the golden fleece from Colchis.

In time, Omphale and Heracles got married. While on a trip to take part in the rites of Bacchus, Heracles slept in a bed made up of Omphale's clothes. The god Pan saw Omphale's clothing and hoped to have relations with the queen, so he crept into her bed, only to find Heracles. The hero was amused by Pan's attempts and threw Pan out of the room.

Shahmaran

One of the most popular and widely celebrated Anatolian mythological figures is Shahmaran, the queen of snakes. According to the myth, Shahmaran was part woman, part snake, and she possessed incredible knowledge of the history of mankind and everlasting life. In the myth, a man named Tahmasp discovered her hiding place. She kept him as a guest to prevent him from telling others about her hiding place and told him fascinating stories. The two eventually fell in love, but Tahmasp longed to return to his family.

Shahmaran understood his desire and allowed him to return to his family on the condition that he never tell anyone about her hiding place and always bathed alone. If he bathed with others, his skin would turn to scales, and people would know that they had been together. Tahmasp agreed and returned home. However, the sultan of his land became sick, and the grand vizier began looking for Shahmaran in an effort to cure the king. The vizier had evil intentions, as he planned to use her knowledge for his own purposes. The vizier passed a law that forbade people from bathing alone, and soon, Tahmasp was caught.

31. Shahmaran

The grand vizier forced Tahmasp to reveal Shahmaran's whereabouts and laid a trap for her. Tahmasp was overcome with guilt, and when they were reunited, he apologized profusely. Shahmaran forgave him. Knowing that the vizier was eavesdropping, she told him that they could cure the king if they killed her, cut up her body, and ate it. She told Tahmasp that whoever ate her body would be healed. Whoever ate her tail would receive wisdom, and whoever ate her head would die.

The vizier immediately revealed himself. He killed Shahmaran, cut her up, and cooked the pieces of her body. He gave the body to the sultan and took the tail for himself. Tahmasp was overcome by guilt and took her head, hoping to die quickly, as he knew he could never forgive himself for betraying Shahmaran. When the sultan ate the body, he was healed. However, when the vizier ate the tail, he died instantly. When Tahmasp ate the head, he received Shahmaran's knowledge. Shahmaran had tricked the grand vizier and ensured that her knowledge went to a worthy candidate. Tahmasp then went on to become the first doctor.

Shahmaran was likely associated with various mother goddesses in Anatolia, and snakes were a popular motif in Anatolian religions, which may have contributed to her enduring popularity.

Chapter 9 – Anatolian Legacy: Emperors and Kings

For better or worse, each ruler of Anatolia helped shape the region. Some emperors and kings left their kingdoms better off than how they had inherited them, while others were responsible for the decline of prosperous and stable nations. For centuries, kingdoms were handed down. Some kings were happy to rule with what they had and barely left a mark at all. However, other kings were ambitious and weren't content to simply rule over what they had inherited. They wanted more and were willing to do anything to get what they wanted. As they conquered new territories, they assimilated new cultures into their own, which led to the development of new and unique cultures.

However, not all would-be conquerors accomplished what they set out to do. Some kings simply flew too close to the sun. These kings wagered everything they had and lost badly, which forever changed the borders of ancient Anatolia. Some of the kings in this chapter managed to turn their kingdoms into empires and were immortalized in myths and legends. Some fell short of their ambitions and became examples to others. While some of these rulers belong in the realm of myths and may have never existed at all, their stories still had an impact on ancient Anatolian culture.

Suppiluliuma I

The Hittite kingdom was one of the most influential ruling powers in Anatolian history. It wasn't always a mighty empire, though. During its earliest periods, it was simply another regional power that struggled to fend off its enemies. All that changed when Suppiluliuma I ascended to the throne. It would seem that the prince's career in the government began when he served as a general under his father, Tudhaliya II. At the time, he was engaged against the Hittite enemies, such as the Kaskians, and the Hittite capital was at Samuha. The young general managed to defeat many of the kingdom's enemies, which likely won him a lot of fame and popularity.

When his father died, his older brother, Tudhaliya III, ascended to the throne, but Suppiluliuma wasn't content to stand by. He overthrew his brother and took the throne for himself around 1344 BCE. This was a disturbing move, and the Hittite priests considered it to be a great crime. It was recorded by his son and biographer, Mursili II. However, Suppiluliuma wasn't going to let that fact hold him back, and he quickly began consolidating his power. He moved the Hittite capital back to Hattusa and began conquering territories. The Mitanni kingdom was conquered by his army and became a Hittite vassal state. Suppiluliuma also forged alliances by taking foreign wives, including a Babylonian princess. Eventually, the Hittite kingdom became a threat to the Egyptians.

When King Tutankhamun of Egypt died, his widow wrote to Suppiluliuma and asked to marry one of his sons. Unfortunately, Suppiluliuma's son died en route to Egypt. (The prince was likely murdered, but the exact details of his death remain a mystery.) Regardless of the circumstances, this enraged the king, who began attacking Egyptian territories. This proved to be a fatal move since many Egyptian prisoners brought the plague with them, which eventually killed Suppiluliuma and his successor, Arnuwanda II, around 1322 BCE. This meant that Suppiluliuma's son, Mursili II, became king instead. Although Mursili II was still young and relatively inexperienced, he managed to prove himself quickly and was a capable king.

Candaules

The kingdom of Lydia was known for being prosperous and having interesting kings. According to the ancient Greek historian Herodotus, Lydia's most notable king was Candaules. Unfortunately, not much is known about Candaules except for what Herodotus wrote about him, which means that historians have to rely on Herodotus's often unreliable testimony. While not everything that Herodotus said was true, historians have at least confirmed that Candaules actually existed. Unfortunately for Candaules, Herodotus's account of the king's rule isn't flattering, and Candaules's name has become a byword for seedy invasions of privacy.

According to Herodotus, Candaules was the last king of the Heraclid dynasty, and he ruled Lydia from the city of Sardis in the 8th century BCE. The ancient legends report that Candaules had an extremely beautiful wife. Candaules was proud of his wife's beauty and forced his servant, Gyges, to spy on the queen while she was naked so that he could get the full measure of her beauty. This proved to be a terrible decision that would lead to Candaules's downfall. The queen spotted Gyges and was terribly embarrassed. She urged Gyges to kill Candaules to preserve her honor. Once Gyges did as the queen asked, he became king.

32. Gyges spying on the queen of Lydia

This story is the most famous account of Candaules's downfall and has been the subject of many paintings. Unfortunately, not much more is known about the ancient king beside the fact that he was the last of the Heraclids. It certainly seems that he suffered a coup at the hands of Gyges, who may have been a member of the king's staff or court. While Candaules's true story is shrouded by mystery, he must have led an eventful life as the king of Lydia and left his mark on Anatolian history as the last Heraclid king. According to the myth, the Lydians weren't happy about Gyges's sudden rise to power, which may have meant that Candaules was at least a capable king, if not a popular one.

Gyges

The Lydian kingdom became one of the richest kingdoms in the world and led the development of coin minting in the west. However, the kingdom became firmly established under the Mermnad dynasty, which was founded by King Gyges. There are many different stories about how Gyges claimed the throne. While Herodotus's account is the most popular, another source states that Gyges used a magical ring that made him invisible to kill the king and then take the queen for himself. A Lydian historian named Xanthus painted Gyges as a disloyal army officer who stole the throne from Candaules. Herodotus claimed that Gyges's actions made him unpopular with the Lydians, which forced him to make a pilgrimage to the Oracle of Delphi. He reportedly promised to give up the throne if the Oracle required it, but apparently, the Oracle supported Gyges's actions, and he was free to rule as he wished.

While the true circumstances regarding Gyges's rise to the throne are unknown, it is clear that Gyges was a competent military leader who increased the borders of the Lydian kingdom. Gyges ascended to the throne around 680 BCE and ruled for about three decades before dying around 652 BCE. He conquered Colophon and Miletus after invading Ionia. Alongside Assyrian King Ashurbanipal, he fought against the Cimmerians. However, he went against the Assyrians when he became involved in an Egyptian uprising. Without his most powerful ally, he was defeated by the Cimmerians, which led to his death.

Ardys

King Ardys rose to the throne after his father, Gyges, was killed by the Cimmerians. In the attack, the capital city, Sardis, was partially destroyed. Ardys became king around 651 BCE. These were difficult circumstances, but Ardys managed to keep control of his kingdom and reportedly went on to become a capable king who contributed to the might of the Mermnad dynasty. Like his father, Ardys mainly focused on military conquests. His first move was to subdue Greek cities to the west, which allowed him to focus on conquering the Cimmerians without worrying about an attack from behind. Afterward, he approached Assyrian King Assurbanipal with a tribute to form an alliance against the Cimmerians.

During this time, the Assyrians were nowhere near as powerful as they had once been, but it seems that they managed to at least push the Cimmerians back. According to Herodotus, Ardys reigned for nearly fifty years, but this doesn't seem to be accurate. While Ardys likely didn't rule that long, he certainly seemed to have had a long and prosperous reign, during which he increased Lydia's borders and wealth. Ardys is also accredited with conquering Priene and fighting against Miletus. However, Miletus was too powerful to conquer, as it had a strong army. Instead of trying to subdue the Milesians, he allowed them some freedoms, such as allowing them to build new cities south of the Black Sea. In return, Miletus was forced to pay tribute to Lydia. This proved to be an astute political move and would have spared both sides the cost of an expensive war.

Ardys was also the first Lydian king who ruled after the fall of the Phrygian kingdom, which would have meant that he ruled during a time of extraordinary change in the region. Unfortunately, Ardys was likely killed when the Cimmerians invaded Lydia and sacked most of Sardis. When he died, he was succeeded by his son, Sadyattes, and buried along with his predecessors at the royal tomb of Bin Tepe.

Alyattes

Alyattes came to the Lydian throne during a time of turmoil that could have cost him the kingship. The Cimmerians proved to be a constant threat to the Lydians and had already sacked the capital of Sardis more than once. Alyattes became king around 610 BCE and faced an uphill battle since he had inherited the responsibility of protecting his kingdom from the Cimmerians. According to Herodotus, Alyattes would be the one who finally defeated the Cimmerians; they supposedly never troubled his kingdom again. However, this didn't lead to peace, as the Mermnad kings had many enemies, including Miletus.

Alyattes continued the Mermnad tradition of visiting the Oracle of Delphi, although he kept attacking Grecian Miletus. This would have been a difficult position for Alyattes. Although he honored many of the Greek gods, he needed the grain that Miletus produced. However, Alyattes didn't let the spiritual dilemma stop him from getting what he needed. In time, he made peace with Miletus, which led to a profitable trading relationship. According to legend, Lydian troops destroyed a temple of Athena in Assesos, which caused the gods to curse Alyattes with an illness. Alyattes was forced to rebuild Athena's temple and make peace with Miletus in order to be cured.

However, it is more likely that the king made peace with Miletus for more profitable reasons. Miletus had plenty of grain but few metal resources, while Lydia had the opposite problem. The peace treaty included clauses that allowed Lydia and Miletus to benefit from the other's resources. Once the terms of the treaty were set, Alyattes turned his attention to the Medes. After five years of fighting, an eclipse occurred, which apparently caused both sides to stop fighting. Alyattes also had to fight against the Carians to the south of Lydia, which he managed to defeat. Later, he went on to conquer the city of Smyrna. He has also been accredited with creating the first electrum coins. When he died, he was buried in a magnificent tomb north of Sardis, which was described by Herodotus and uncovered by archaeologists in 1854 CE.

Croesus

Croesus succeeded his father, Alyattes, to the throne around 560 BCE and became one of the wealthiest kings in the world. He became so prosperous that his name remains a byword for wealth even in modern times. According to legend (of which there are plenty involving Croesus), the king became rich from the Pactolus River, which was filled with gold because King Midas had washed in the river to rid himself of a gift bestowed on him by the god Dionysus. While many of the stories regarding Croesus are mythical, historians have confirmed that he was a real king who ruled Lydia from the capital of Sardis. Croesus may have funded the construction of the Temple of Artemis, which was a spectacular building that became one of the Seven Wonders of the Ancient World. Herodotus was one of the foremost experts on Croesus and wrote several famous stories about the king.

33. Croesus and Solon

According to Herodotus, Croesus received a visit from Solon, a famous wise man from Athens. Croesus was happy to show off his wealth to Solon and reportedly asked him who the happiest man on earth was. Solon answered, "Tellus of Athens." Croesus was disappointed and asked why Solon chose to name Tellus instead of him. Solon answered that Tellus had died for Athens in battle and had a beautiful family. Croesus admitted that Tellus sounded like a good man, so he asked Solon who was the happiest man he had ever met. Solon responded that Cleobis and Biton were the happiest because they had lived and died well. Croesus lost his temper with Solon and asked why he hadn't been named, and Solon calmly replied that a man could only be called happy after living and dying well.

Croesus was angry with Solon's answer and decided to dismiss the wise man's words. Later, his son, Atys, died while hunting a boar. After grieving Atys's death, Croesus received word that the Persians were going to attack his kingdom. In response, he consulted the Oracle of Delphi, who prophesied that Croesus would destroy a great empire if he went to war. Croesus took that to mean that he would win the war against the Persians. Unfortunately, Croesus was defeated by Cyrus the Great.

According to legend, Cyrus ordered that Croesus should be burned alive on a pyre. Croesus called out to Apollo for help, and he was saved. However, he was still Cyrus's prisoner. During this time, he remembered Solon's prediction that a man could only be counted happy after his death. He also realized that the Oracle's prophecy had come true but that he had misinterpreted her words. After all, it was true that a great empire had fallen, except it was Lydia that had been destroyed.

Some sources claim that Cyrus took pity on Croesus and kept him as a wise man in his court. However, others state that Croesus was carried away by Apollo after Sardis fell and lived in peace with his family. While there are several accounts of how Croesus died, he was still the last king of Lydia, and the empire never recovered after it was defeated by Cyrus.

Gordias

Phrygia was surely one of the greatest kingdoms of ancient Anatolia before its complete defeat. One of the most famous myths about Phrygia involves one of its first kings, Gordias, who would leave behind a legacy that endured until Alexander the Great reached Anatolia. Even then, he left a lasting mark on Anatolian history.

According to the myth, Gordias was a peasant who was working in his fields when an eagle landed on his plow and stayed there all day. Gordias realized that it was an omen and consulted the Telmessians, who were ancient prophets. A Telmessian woman who was standing in a doorway advised Gordias to make an offering to Zeus. Gordias obeyed her and then went on his way. In time, he got married and had a son named Midas.

One day, while Midas was traveling with his father's wagon to the city of Gordium, he noticed that the city was being torn apart by civil war. Midas entered the city, and the people immediately named him king. Apparently, the people had been told by an oracle that a man would enter the city on a wagon and end the war by becoming the king of Phrygia. In many versions of the story, Gordias became the king, and his son succeeded him.

The legend goes on to state that Gordias tied his wagon with an incredibly intricate knot and claimed that whoever undid the knot would go on to rule the whole world or all of Asia (it depends on the version). The knot and wagon remained outside of the temple of Zeus until the arrival of the Macedonian king, Alexander the Great, who was on his way to fight a war against Persia. In some variations of the story, Alexander simply removed the pin from the knot and unhitched the wagon, while in others, he grew impatient with the knot and cut it with his sword.

Not much is known about the real Gordias, but it is clear that the Phrygian kingship was strongly connected to divine approval. It also connects to the Phrygian religious imagery of a mother goddess, as she was usually depicted as standing in a doorway.

Priam

The ancient city of Troy has been immortalized in mythology and art. It has provided powerful imagery that has been used in various artworks for centuries. According to Greek mythology, Priam was the last king of Troy before the city was conquered, and he faced many hardships that eventually broke his strong spirit.

Homer's *Iliad* states that he inherited the throne from his father, Laomedon, and was a capable king who had several wives and fifty sons, including Hector and Paris. Paris went on to cause the Trojan War by stealing Helen away from her husband, Menelaus, the king of Sparta. By the time the war began, Priam was an old man who was long past his prime. He was also a kind man who didn't blame Helen for what had happened and relied heavily on his sons to fight the war. The war dragged on for many years, and Priam suffered heavy casualties, including the loss of thirteen of his sons. The final blow came when Achilles killed three of Priam's sons—Polydorus, Lycaon, and Hector—in one day.

Hector's death was the loss that finally broke Priam's heart since Hector was Troy's last hope. Priam bravely faced Achilles and paid to have Hector's corpse returned to him. Troy finally fell after the Greeks left a wooden horse containing hidden warriors at the Trojan's gate. Priam was killed on an altar by Achilles' son, Neoptolemus.

34. The Death of Priam

Like many Anatolian kings who were shrouded in myth, not much is known about Priam except what was recorded in Greek mythology. The stories paint him as a kind man and a capable king who endured terrible losses before his eventual defeat.

Conclusion

Ancient Anatolia is surrounded by myth and mystery. Most of its secrets have yet to be uncovered by scholars, and what is known is wrapped in legend. From the time that mankind roved about in nomadic tribes to times when fabled kings built influential empires, Anatolia was inhabited by extraordinary people who developed elaborate belief systems. They also left behind magnificent pieces of art that identify their civilizations and tell stories of gods, heroes, and monsters.

The first chapter of this book delved into the history of Göbekli Tepe, which may have been mankind's first cathedral on a hill. Much of its allure is due to its age and mysterious purpose and origins. The next chapter discussed other early Anatolian settlements. As people began to settle down and make homes for themselves in Anatolia, they built complex civilizations. Their homes may have had cooling systems, and people created artwork to decorate their homes and pay honor to their gods. While they didn't leave behind any written records, they left behind a multitude of clues that give us insight into what their lives were like.

In time, powerful kingdoms emerged in Anatolia and began consolidating their power. Civilizations like the Hittites and Mitanni united or conquered indigenous tribes, which they then assimilated into their own cultures. As a result, most Anatolian cultures bear influences from their predecessors and neighbors. Each culture is unique and fascinating, but most are linked to each other in one way or another. After a lengthy power struggle, the Hittites defeated the Mitanni and became an unstoppable power that threatened some of the most established empires of its time. However, when the Hittites were defeated, new kingdoms flourished in their place.

This led to a classical period in Anatolian history that featured three notable kingdoms: Phrygia, Lydia, and Urartu. Lydia was renowned for its wealth, and its kings came up with an ingenious coinage system that was quickly adopted by its neighbors. The kingdom's wealth increased under the Mermnad dynasty, which relied heavily on the Oracle of Delphi. They acquired so much wealth that stories of their prosperity reached legendary status. Unfortunately, due to a misinterpreted prophecy, the kingdom was conquered by Cyrus the Great. While Phrygia fell long before the Lydians, their kings played a role in several Greek myths. Their art, religion, and culture still hold interest today, which is a testament to their influence and capabilities. Urartu was another mysterious kingdom that posed a threat to the Assyrians and left behind a distinct artistic heritage. They were known for being brave warriors, adept horsemen, and capable farmers who skillfully used their fertile lands to the fullest.

Finally, the last part of this book focused on the art, architecture, and archaeological history of many ancient Anatolian cultures. The kingdoms of Anatolia had close ties with each other. When they weren't fighting each other, they were trading and sharing knowledge with one another. Thus, these cultures influenced each other and were often closely related. The motifs and themes that were popular in ancient Anatolia spilled over to later cultures that used Anatolian themes in their own works. And while many ancient Anatolian cultures didn't leave behind many written records, their art and inscriptions reveal their religious systems, which often consisted of pantheons of gods and goddesses who represented certain ideals. For instance, the Urartians were headed by the god of war, while the Phrygians and Lydians worshiped many Greek gods. Most Anatolian cultures shared common religious themes, such as mother goddesses. Their mythology featured a mix of uniquely Anatolian characters as well as Greek heroes, such as Heracles.

The last chapter of this book took a look at some of the most influential kings and conquerors in Anatolian history. Some of them can be verified by historical sources and left behind inscriptions recording their deeds. They changed the course of Anatolian history by either starting new dynasties or bringing an end to their kingdom. Others were powerful figures who inspired the myths and legends that still define them. Their exploits have a firm place in the public imagination, even though their true stories have been lost to time.

A lot can be learned from the remnants of these cultures. While scholars might never know exact details or find comprehensive written records left behind by these cultures, their artifacts still have a lot of stories to tell. In time, the Roman and Byzantine Empires imposed their will on Anatolia, but ancient Anatolian cultures had already left a distinct mark on the region. These cultures and civilizations certainly had a hand in the modern cultures that inhabit the Republic of Turkey, and they still have many treasures to reveal.

Here's another book by Captivating History that you might like

Free Bonus from Captivating History (Available for a Limited time)

Hi History Lovers!

Now you have a chance to join our exclusive history list so you can get your first history ebook for free as well as discounts and a potential to get more history books for free! Simply visit the link below to join.

Captivatinghistory.com/ebook

Also, make sure to follow us on Facebook, Twitter and Youtube by searching for Captivating History.

Bibliography

Information Sources:

Title: Göbekli Tepe: The World's First Temple?

    Date Accessed: 14/3/22

    Link: https://www.smithsonianmag.com/history/gobekli-tepe-the-worlds-first-temple-83613665/

Title: Göbekli Tepe

    Date Accessed: 14/3/22

    Link: https://www.worldhistory.org/G%C3%B6bekli_Tepe/

Title: World's Oldest Temple to Be Restored

    Date Accessed: 14/3/22

    Link: https://www.nationalgeographic.com/travel/article/150120-gobekli-tepe-oldest-monument-turkey-archaeology

Title: Turkey: Conservation, not excavation, focus in Gobeklitepe

    Date Accessed: 17/3/22

    Link: https://www.aa.com.tr/en/culture/turkey-conservation-not-excavation-focus-in-gobeklitepe/1758455

Title: Neolithic Period in Anatolia

    Date Accessed: 17/3/22

    Link: https://libguides.ku.edu.tr/anatoliancivilizations/neolithicchalcolithicanatolia

Title: The Neolithic Period

Date Accessed: 17/3/22

Link: https://www.britannica.com/place/Anatolia/The-Neolithic-Period

Title: What Happened to Turkey's Ancient Utopia?

Date Accessed: 17/3/22

Link: https://www.discovermagazine.com/the-sciences/what-happened-to-turkeys-ancient-utopia

Title: Early Places Without Metals: Nevali Cori

Date Accessed: 17/3/22

Link: https://www.tf.uni-kiel.de/matwis/amat/iss/kap_a/advanced/ta_1_2g.html

Title: Eastern Anatolia in the Chalcolithic and Early Bronze Age

Date Accessed: 17/3/22

Link: https://www.jstor.org/stable/3642418

Title: Anatolian art and Architecture

Date Accessed: 17/3/22

Link: https://www.britannica.com/art/Anatolian-art#ref419800

Title: Early Bronze Age

Date Accessed: 17/3/22

Link: https://www.britannica.com/place/Anatolia/Early-Bronze-Age

Title: The Kura-Araxes Culture from the Caucasus to Iran, Anatolia and the Levant: Between unity and diversity. A synthesis

Date Accessed: 17/3/22

Link: https://www.persee.fr/doc/paleo_0153-9345_2014_num_40_2_5645

Title: Hatti

Date Accessed: 17/3/22

Link: https://www.worldhistory.org/hatti/

Title: Between the states: Iron Age interaction in southwestern Anatolia

Date Accessed: 17/3/22

Link: https://www.sciencedirect.com/science/article/abs/pii/S2352409X15300183

Title: Yarimburgaz Cave Monastery

Date Accessed: 18/3/22

Link: https://www.thebyzantinelegacy.com/yarimburgaz

Title: The Hittites and Ancient Anatolia

Date Accessed: 24/3/22

Link: https://www.khanacademy.org/humanities/world-history/world-history-beginnings/ancient-egypt-hittites/a/the-hittites#:~:text=Overview,government%2C%20and%20worshipped%20storm%20gods.

Title: The Hittites

Date Accessed: 24/3/22

Link: https://www.worldhistory.org/hittite/

Title: The Battle of Kadesh & the First Peace Treaty

Date Accessed: 24/3/22

Link: https://www.worldhistory.org/article/78/the-battle-of-kadesh--the-first-peace-treaty/

Title: Mitanni

Date Accessed: 24/3/22

Link: https://www.worldhistory.org/Mitanni/

Title: Mitanni

Date Accessed: 24/3/22

Link: https://www.britannica.com/place/Mitanni

Title: Lydia

Date Accessed: 28/3/22

Link: https://www.worldhistory.org/lydia/

Title: Lydia

Date Accessed: 28/3/22

Link: https://www.britannica.com/place/Lydia-ancient-region-Anatolia

Title: The Myth of the Lydia Empire

Date Accessed: 28/3/22

Link:https://www.researchgate.net/publication/280903152_The_Myth_of_the_Lydian_Empire

Title: Herodotus on Lydia

Date Accessed: 28/3/22

Link: https://www.worldhistory.org/article/81/herodotus-on-lydia/

Title: Mermnad dynasty

Date Accessed: 28/3/22

Link: https://www.livius.org/articles/dynasty/mermnads/

Title: Sardis

Date Accessed: 28/3/22

Link: https://www.worldhistory.org/sardis/

Title: Arachne

Date Accessed: 28/3/22

Link: https://www.britannica.com/topic/Arachne

Title: The Lydians and their Ionian and Aeolian Neighbors

Date Accessed: 29/3/22

Link: https://sardisexpedition.org/en/essays/latw-kerschner-lydians-ionian-neighbors

Title: Ionia

Date Accessed: 29/3/22

Link: https://www.worldhistory.org/ionia/

Title: Phrygia

Date Accessed: 29/3/22

Link: https://www.britannica.com/place/Phrygia

Title: Phrygia

Date Accessed: 29/3/22

Link: https://www.worldhistory.org/phrygia/

Title: Dactyls

Date Accessed: 29/3/22

Link: https://www.encyclopedia.com/science/encyclopedias-almanacs-transcripts-and-maps/dactyls

Title: Gordium

Date Accessed: 29/3/22

Link: https://www.worldhistory.org/Gordium/

Title: Midas

    Date Accessed: 29/3/22

    Link: https://www.britannica.com/topic/Midas-Greek-mythology

Title: Cimmerians

    Date Accessed: 29/3/22

    Link: https://iranicaonline.org/articles/cimmerians-nomads

Title: The History of Herodotus

    Date Accessed: 29/3/22

    Link: http://classics.mit.edu/Herodotus/history.2.ii.html

Title: Trojan War

    Date Accessed: 29/3/22

    Link: https://www.britannica.com/event/Trojan-War

Title: Adrastus

    Date Accessed: 29/3/22

    Link:http://www.perseus.tufts.edu/hopper/text?doc=Perseus%3Atext%3A1999.04.0104%3Aalphabetic+letter%3DA%3Aentry+group%3D5%3Aentry%3Dadrastus-bio-2

Title: Urartu Civilization

    Date Accessed: 30/3/22

    Link: https://www.worldhistory.org/Urartu_Civilization/

Title: Urartu

    Date Accessed: 30/3/22

    Link: https://www.britannica.com/place/Urartu

Title: Winning Against the Odds: Sargon II & the Urartu Campaign

    Date Accessed: 30/3/22

    Link: https://www.worldhistory.org/article/727/winning-against-the-odds-sargon-ii--the-urartu-cam/

Title: Necropolis in Turkey Reveals the Iron Age Burial Customs of the Urartu

    Date Accessed: 30/3/22

    Link: https://www.ancient-origins.net/news-history-archaeology/necropolis-turkey-reveals-iron-age-burial-customs-urartu-0015853

Title: Anatolian Art and architecture

Date Accessed: 3/4/22

Link: https://www.britannica.com/art/Anatolian-art/Middle-Bronze-Age

Title: Alaca Hüyük

Date Accessed: 3/4/22

Link: https://www.britannica.com/place/Alaca-Huyuk

Title: Considering the re-use of late bronze age buildings in light of contextual information and human remains at Beycesultan

Date Accessed: 3/4/22

Link: https://www.researchgate.net/publication/301788601_Considering_the_re-use_of_late_bronze_age_buildings_in_light_of_contextual_information_and_human_remains_at_beycesultan

Title: Priam's Treasure

Date Accessed: 3/4/22

Link: https://www.britannica.com/topic/Priams-Treasure

Title: Bronze and Iron: Ancient Near Eastern Artifacts in the Metropolitan Museum of Art

Date Accessed: 3/4/22

Link: https://books.google.co.za/books?id=5sxqNhfmcQUC&pg=PA395&lpg=PA395&dq=horoztepe+and+mahmatlar&source=bl&ots=e9u7NsKSMg&sig=ACfU3U1Ln3wopvZtNY5Xt8UCJ3PF15yJcg&hl=en&sa=X&ved=2ahUKEwj81tGZpPj2AhVxQkEAHeUnC-0Q6AF6BAgVEAM#v=onepage&q=horoztepe%20and%20mahmatlar&f=false

Title: Hatti Civilization

Date Accessed: 3/4/22

Link: https://www.allaboutturkey.com/hatti.html

Title: Hatti (Hattusa)

Date Accessed: 3/4/22

Link: https://www.historyfiles.co.uk/KingListsMiddEast/AnatoliaHattiHattusa.htm

Title: Kültepe

Date Accessed: 3/4/22

Link: https://www.britannica.com/place/Kultepe

Title: Hittite Art and Architecture

Date Accessed: 3/4/22

Link: https://www.encyclopedia.com/reference/encyclopedias-almanacs-transcripts-and-maps/hittite-art-and-architecture

Title: Syro-Hittite Monumental Art and the Archaeology of Performance

Date Accessed: 3/4/22

Link: https://www.researchgate.net/publication/281626535_Syro-Hittite_Monumental_Art_and_the_Archaeology_of_Performance

Title: Urartu Art

Date Accessed: 3/4/22

Link: https://www.worldhistory.org/Urartu_Art/

Title: Phrygia

Date Accessed: 3/4/22

Link: https://www.allaboutturkey.com/phrygia.html

Title: Lydian Art

Date Accessed: 3/4/22

Link: http://www.about-turkey.com/karun/art.htm

Title: Objects from Horoztepe

Date Accessed: 4/4/22

Link: https://belleten.gov.tr/tam-metin-pdf/2992/eng

Title: Religions of the Hittites, Hattians, and Hurrians

Date Accessed: 4/4/22

Link: https://www.britannica.com/topic/Anatolian-religion/Religions-of-the-Hittites-Hattians-and-Hurrians#ref559576

Title: The Hittite Religion

Date Accessed: 4/4/22

Link: https://www.allaboutturkey.com/hittite-gods.html#:~:text=The%20religion%20of%20the%20Hittite,suggesting%20an%20early%20matrilineal%20society.

Title: The Gods of Lydia

Date Accessed: 4/4/22

Link: https://sardisexpedition.org/en/essays/latw-greenewalt-gods-of-lydia#:~:text=Lydian%20religion%20was%20polytheistic%2C%20with,were%20partly%20or%20wholly%20Greek.

Title: Urartu Religion

Date Accessed: 4/4/22

Link: https://www.worldhistory.org/Urartu_Religion/

Title: Tantalus

Date Accessed: 4/4/22

Link:https://www.worldhistory.org/Tantalus/#:~:text=Definition&text=Tantalus%20is%20a%20figure%20from,reach%20of%20a%20fruit%20tree.

Title: Midas

Date Accessed: 4/4/22

Link: https://www.worldhistory.org/midas/

Title: Hittite Online

Date Accessed: 4/4/22

Link:https://lrc.la.utexas.edu/eieol/hitol/20#:~:text=The%20Telepenus%20Myth%20is%20one,dire%20consequences%20for%20that%20world.

Title: The Anatolian Myth of Illuyanka

Date Accessed: 4/4/22

Link:https://www.researchgate.net/publication/280224007_The_Anatolian_Myth_of_Illuyanka

Title: Hercules and Omphale

Date Accessed: 4/4/22

Link: https://www.marcmaison.com/architectural-antiques-resources/hercules-and-omphale

Title: The Queen of Serpents and the Mythical Doctor

Date Accessed: 4/4/22

Link: http://anatolianstories.blogspot.com/2014/06/the-queen-of-serpents-and-mythical.html

Title: Cybele

Date Accessed: 4/4/22

Link: https://www.worldhistory.org/Cybele/

Title: Gyges

Date Accessed: 5/4/22

Link: https://www.britannica.com/biography/Gyges

Title: Croesus

Date Accessed: 5/4/22

Link: https://www.worldhistory.org/croesus/

Title: King Candaules of the Ancient Greek Kingdom of Lydia

Date Accessed: 5/4/22

Link: https://www.greekboston.com/culture/ancient-history/king-candaules/

Title: Ardys of Lydia

Date Accessed: 5/4/22

Link: https://www.livius.org/articles/person/ardys/

Title: Alyattes

Date Accessed: 5/4/22

Link: https://www.britannica.com/biography/Alyattes

Title: The Gordian Knot

Date Accessed: 5/4/22

Link: https://www.penn.museum/sites/gordion/articles/myth-religion/the-gordian-knot/

Title: Could Rusa son of Erimena have been king of Urartu during Sargon's Eighth Campaign?

Date Accessed: 5/4/22

Link: https://www.academia.edu/30995381/Could_Rusa_son_of_Erimena_have_been_king_of_Urartu_during_Sargon_s_Eighth_Campaign_

Title: The Kingdom of Van (Urartu)

    Date Accessed: 5/4/22

    Link: http://www.attalus.org/armenian/kvan2.htm

Title: Suppililiumas I

    Date Accessed: 5/4/22

    Link: https://www.britannica.com/biography/Suppiluliumas-I

Title: Priam

    Date Accessed: 5/4/22

    Link: https://www.britannica.com/topic/Priam-Greek-mythology

Title: Urartu

    Date Accessed: 5/4/22

    Link: https://www.britannica.com/place/Urartu#ref279174

Title: The Deeds of Suppiluliuma as Told by His Son, Mursili II

    Date Accessed: 5/4/22

    Link:

    https://www.jstor.org/stable/1359041?read-now=1&refreqid=excelsior%3Ad6e63d5ef8084d645b96da7a426eb78d&seq=9

Picture Sources:

5. Creative Commons: Attribution- CeeGee, CC BY-SA 4.0
https://creativecommons.org/licenses/by-sa/4.0 , via Wikimedia Commons;
https://commons.wikimedia.org/wiki/File:Yar%C4%B1mburgazCave_(10).JPG.

6. Creative Commons: Attribution- Dosseman, CC BY-SA 4.0
https://creativecommons.org/licenses/by-sa/4.0 , via Wikimedia Commons;
https://commons.wikimedia.org/wiki/File:Urfa_museum_Neval%C4%B1_%C3%87
ori_Temple_-_Neolithic_age_4844.jpg.

7. Creative Commons: Attribution- Murat Özsoy 1958, CC BY-SA 4.0
https://creativecommons.org/licenses/by-sa/4.0 , via Wikimedia Commons;
https://commons.wikimedia.org/wiki/File:%C3%87atalh%C3%B6y%C3%BCk,_740
0_BC,_Konya,_Turkey_-_UNESCO_World_Heritage_Site,_10.jpg.

8. Creative Commons: Attribution- Kober, CC BY-SA 4.0
https://creativecommons.org/licenses/by-sa/4.0 , via Wikimedia Commons;
https://commons.wikimedia.org/wiki/File:Sighnaghi_Museum._Bronze_Age_pottery
_and_bronze_axe.jpg.

9. Creative Commons: Attribution- Carole Raddato from FRANKFURT, Germany,
CC BY-SA 2.0 https://creativecommons.org/licenses/by-sa/2.0 , via Wikimedia
Commons;
https://commons.wikimedia.org/wiki/File:Necklace_found_in_one_of_the_Hattian_
graves_in_Alacah%C3%B6y%C3%BCk,_2500-
2250_BC,_Museum_of_Anatolian_Civilizations,_Ankara_(28619225602).jpg.

10. Public domain;
https://commons.wikimedia.org/wiki/File:The_Hittites_-
_Slabs_with_Hittite_Sculptures_found_at_Keller_near_Aintab.png.

11. Creative Commons: Attribution- Nicoleon, CC BY-SA 4.0
https://creativecommons.org/licenses/by-sa/4.0 , via Wikimedia Commons;
https://commons.wikimedia.org/wiki/File:SUPPILULIUMA.jpg.

12. Creative Commons: Attribution- Roland Unger, CC BY-SA 3.0
https://creativecommons.org/licenses/by-sa/3.0 , via Wikimedia Commons;
https://commons.wikimedia.org/wiki/File:AbydosR2QadeshBattle-81.jpg.

13. Creative Commons: Attribution- Metropolitan Museum of Art, CC0, via
Wikimedia

Commons;
https://commons.wikimedia.org/wiki/File:Cylinder_seal,_ca._1500%E2%80%93135
0_BC_Mitanni.jpg.

14. Creative Commons: Attribution- Bernard Gagnon, CC BY-SA 3.0
https://creativecommons.org/licenses/by-sa/3.0 , via Wikimedia Commons;
https://commons.wikimedia.org/wiki/File:Lion_Gate,_Hattusa_01.jpg.

15. Creative Commons: Attribution- O.Mustafin, CC0, via Wikimedia Commons;
https://commons.wikimedia.org/wiki/File:Lydian_coin.jpg.

16. Public domain;
https://commons.wikimedia.org/wiki/File:Alexander_cuts_the_Gordian_Knot.jpg.

17. Public domain; https://commons.wikimedia.org/wiki/File:The_trojan_horse.jpg.

18. Public domain; https://commons.wikimedia.org/wiki/File:Urartu_Chariot.jpg.

19. Creative Commons: Attribution- gozturk, CC BY 3.0
https://creativecommons.org/licenses/by/3.0 , via Wikimedia Commons;
https://commons.wikimedia.org/wiki/File:Akhtamar_Island_on_Lake_Van_with_th
e_Armenian_Cathedral_of_the_Holy_Cross.jpg.

20. Public domain;
https://commons.wikimedia.org/wiki/File:Priam%27s_treasure.jpg#file.

21. Creative Commons: Attribution- Stipich Béla, CC BY-SA 3.0
http://creativecommons.org/licenses/by-sa/3.0/ , via Wikimedia Commons;
https://commons.wikimedia.org/wiki/File:Alaca_H%C3%BCy%C3%BCk_1.jpg

22. Creative Commons: Attribution- Ingeborg Simon, CC BY-SA 3.0
https://creativecommons.org/licenses/by-sa/3.0 , via Wikimedia Commons;
https://commons.wikimedia.org/wiki/File:Beycesultan_16.jpg.

23. Creative Commons: Attribution- Bjørn Christian Tørrissen, CC BY-SA 3.0
https://creativecommons.org/licenses/by-sa/3.0 , via Wikimedia Commons;
https://commons.wikimedia.org/wiki/File:Horoztepe_Mother_Bronze.JPG.

24. Creative Commons: Attribution- Ur-Pabilsag, CC BY-SA 4.0
https://creativecommons.org/licenses/by-sa/4.0 , via Wikimedia Commons;
https://commons.wikimedia.org/wiki/File:Hittite_Priest-King_or_Deity.jpg.

25. Creative Commons: Attribution- Cleveland Museum of Art, CC0, via
Wikimedia

Commons;
https://commons.wikimedia.org/wiki/File:Urartian,_northwest_Iran,_possibly_Gus%C3%A7i,_Lake_Urmia,_c._700-600_BC_-_Bull_Head_Attachment_-_1942.204_-_Cleveland_Museum_of_Art.tif.

26. Creative Commons: Attribution- Israel Museum, CC0, via Wikimedia Commons;
https://commons.wikimedia.org/wiki/File:Clay_Vessel_Painted_with_Winged_Monster,_Phrygia_(Turkey),_8th-7th_Century_BC_(41409568350).jpg.

27. Creative Commons: Attribution- Dosseman, CC BY-SA 4.0

https://creativecommons.org/licenses/by-sa/4.0 , via Wikimedia Commons;

https://commons.wikimedia.org/wiki/File:U%C5%9Fak_Museum_Lydian_gold_objects_and_their_moulds_2179.jpg.

28. Creative Commons: Attribution- British Museum, CC BY-SA 2.0 FR

https://creativecommons.org/licenses/by-sa/2.0/fr/deed.en , via Wikimedia Commons;

https://commons.wikimedia.org/wiki/File:Storm_god-1926.0219.1-IMG_3906-gradient.jpg.

29. Creative Commons: Attribution- Bujomar, CC BY-SA 4.0

https://creativecommons.org/licenses/by-sa/4.0 , via Wikimedia Commons;

https://commons.wikimedia.org/wiki/File:Cyb%C3%A8le_Potnia_theron.jpg.

30. Public domain; https://commons.wikimedia.org/wiki/File:TournierMidas.jpg.

31. Creative Commons: Attribution- MikaelF derivative work:Gomada, CC BY-SA 2.0 https://creativecommons.org/licenses/by-sa/2.0 , via Wikimedia Commons;

https://commons.wikimedia.org/wiki/File:%C5%9Eahmaran.jpg.

32. Public domain;

https://commons.wikimedia.org/wiki/File:William_Etty_(1787%E2%80%931849)_%E2%80%93_Candaules,_King_of_Lydia,_Shews_his_Wife_by_Stealth_to_Gyges,_One_of_his_Ministers,_as_She_Goes_to_Bed_%E2%80%93_N00358_%E2%80%93_Tate.jpg.

33. Public domain;

https://commons.wikimedia.org/wiki/File:Honthorst_solon_and_croesus.jpg.

34. Public domain;
https://commons.wikimedia.org/wiki/File:Jean_Baptiste_Regnault_-_The_Death_of_Priam,_1785.jpg.

Made in the USA
Las Vegas, NV
05 June 2023

72994239R00077